POPOGROU ANTHOLOGY

Poetry from the
POPOGROU COLLECTIVE

POPOGROU ANTHOLOGY

Poetry from the
POPOGROU COLLECTIVE

EDITED BY SIMON TYRRELL

KU
PRESS

KINGSTON UNIVERSITY
PRESS

ISBN 978-1-909362-79-6

Typeset in Baskerville, Avenir and Hiragino Kaku Gothic std.

Photographs/artwork © the individual creators.

Cover illustration by Alana Applewhaite.
Editorial and design by Alana Applewhaite, Kara Daniel, Emma Fisher and Julieta Pereyra.

KINGSTON UNIVERSITY PRESS
Kingston University
Penrhyn Road
Kingston-upon-Thames
KT1 2EE

Contents

INTRODUCTION

The potential poetry group is a book that is a group of people that are poets that are making authentic typically eccentric innovations in literature while are being uniformly and mindfully kind and generous and amiable while meeting each other often at performance events and exhibitions and walks and most vitally at workshop sessions that most often take place three times a year and on wednesday evenings on a zoom after the pandemic and have happened maybe something like ten times at the time of writing but I am guessing it could be more but why check what does it matter but if it has been ten times which it definitely has then that's sixty meetings and i'd say it's more than that i'd say probably one hundred meetings with three hundred presentations of work by poets who are doing the kind of thing that each value and are inspired because it is what that person presenting is truly at and with and in for they have discovered for themselves that the quality of being good at poetry is rendering away all blockages before a kind of instinct and trusting that while doing so with one's feet in the soil and then with a sense of playfulness of humour of exploration of curiosity of inquisitiveness and difference true difference for that must come from an authentic attempt to make what one wants to make is it coming out different but without fully meaning this word that individuality carrying something universal or rather in this case collective and that then making real friendships really bonding human poets together into a kind of dare i say family and this then unblood family going on sharing supporting growing opening up and making work always new books performance collaborations taking on the visual in poetry the sonic the photographic cinematic conceptual textual semantic and doing all that without really much architecture of theory too just a friendly and expressive immediacy a sincerity that helps understanding and all of this being let's face it quite miraculous for how do people find each other in this world in this way it cannot be planned or aimed for or sought after it can only happen by accident and then be seized upon and this with all the brilliant brilliant poetry which makes others think how good is this person and how good can people be then also how happy and aware everyone involved in this group is of how special popogrou is and how rare and how it has become something that makes nearly twenty people's lives better and should be one day studied as a really important literary movement but probably won't because that is the way of the world that the really complex and interesting is just for those who are in it and of it and maybe that is the better way of it unless you are reading this and are not connected to the group well then you are doing the real work thanks so much for reading and thanks for simon for editing this book and thanks for everyone involved in popogrou from me who kind of founded it and i am happy to say that because i am so proud of the group and what it is and being associated with everyone in it glowing and the works that follow will speak of all this in a less clearer way than this crystal clear introduction which is better representative of what can't be captured anyway which is the hours spent in the company of a grand set of poets who loosely collect under eight letters

sj fowler 2024

LISA
BLACKWELL

Lisa Blackwell writes poetry, fiction and plays. Her poetry has been published by *The Rialto*, *3:AM Magazine*, Broken Sleep Books and Shearsman. Her first poetry pamphlet *How it will Happen* is the Three Trees Portfolio Award winner in 2022, and is out now with Maytree Press.

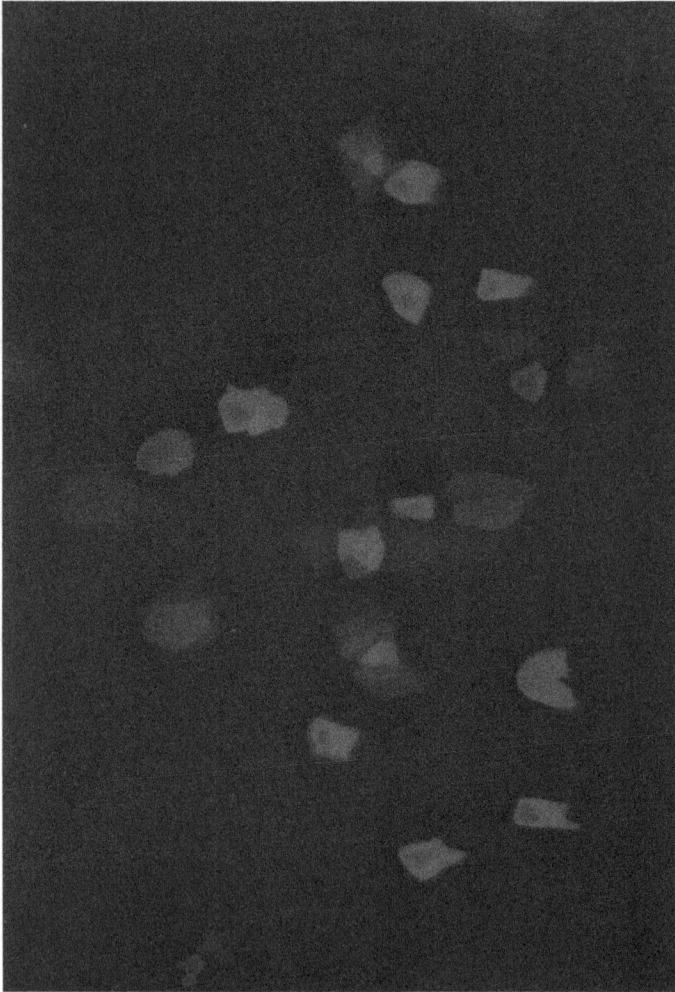

Lumenprint of baby teeth

Thesis resist monkeys

is what my phone's autocorrect tells me I mean, when I try to write about thesis monkeys. Fucking bastard autocorrect: it's at it again. Rhesus monkeys. I can't actually see what I'm typing as I have my contact lenses in.

Scientists had two fake mummy monkeys. One furry without food, one made of steel with food. The monkey baby would cling to the furry monkey mummy until it got too hungry. Then it would go to the steel monkey mummy, get food, then straight back to cuddly monkey mummy.

The underground is advertising skin-toned condoms called *Roam*. Apparently they *set the right tone. Perfectly balanced for sensation and safety. Challenging the status quo.* Hectoring condoms are making my mojo feel very sad.

The man on the train is telling a story about how he cried his eyes out when he started school. He looks about 60. The teacher told his mum, *Don't worry he'll be alright in a minute.* They always say that, whether it's true or not.

Lumenprint of baby curl

They said it to me when I left my son his first day at school. His small face contorted at the window. Mums patting my upper arm as I walked away sobbing. *All my life*, the man continues, *and my mother's life*. He looks off into the distance shaking his head unable to continue.

There was once a rapper who leant so far out of his SUV to pick up his jacket potato that had fallen on to the ground, that he half fell out of the SUV and half ran himself over. Apparently, he was quite seriously injured.

My bones still whimper from the beating.

The woman sitting opposite me on the Tube has just said vehemently to the woman next to her: *I don't like things that spin*. She doesn't specify whether she means roundabouts, washing machines or the Earth. One's fun, one's functional and one is the system that supports all life.

One should not be embarrassed of one's own body. Given to us by nature.

The man next to me on the Tube has his shirt sleeves rolled up, and I'm keeping an eye on the dark hairs and mole on his right forearm. It all looks a bit lively.

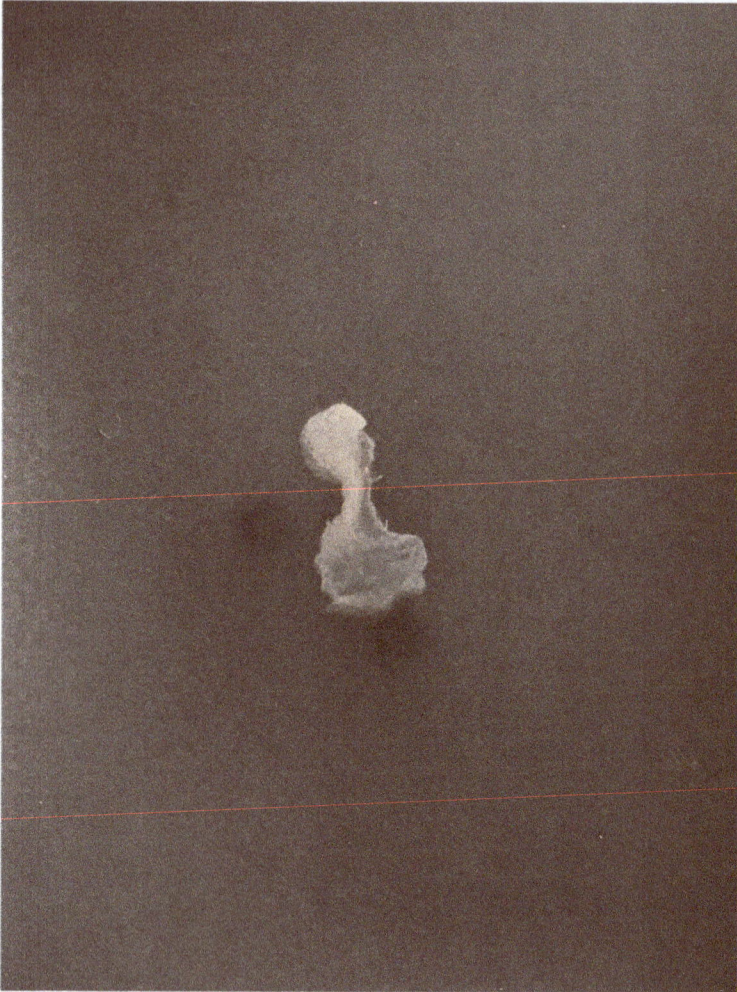

Lumenprint of fragment of umbilical cord

Things seem to be moving when they should be keeping still. He's watching the *Simpsons* on his phone but doesn't seem to be paying much attention. I am very suspicious. I remember being told about lizard people but I can't remember what it was. I would like to leave, but it's not my stop and I'm feeling a bit belligerent that I shouldn't be chased away by some hairs and a mole. So I stay.

The woman on the train in the seat in front, has just said to her boyfriend, *I got the vision, I just aint got the energy.*

One time the scientists created a cuddly monkey mummy that would shoot a jet of air at the baby rhesus monkey when it tried to cuddle the monkey mummy. This would distress the monkey baby. And the more the monkey mummy abused the monkey baby, the more the monkey baby tried to cuddle the fake abusive monkey mummy. And so on and so forth. Until the monkey baby could no longer function it was so distressed.

Some things are just so fundamentally wrong that it makes you wish for thesis resist monkeys.

The Popogrou Collective is a community of humans working in the margins of poetry and art and everything that is today and yesterday and tomorrow and tomorrow and tomorrow.

There are no rules for Popogrou and no Manifesto/Womanifesta. Or perhaps there is but no one has told me what they are. Quite possibly, everyone has their own rules for Popogrou, which is the Popogrou way (if there was a way, which there is not).

It is words and art and noise and jumping in a bush. It is noticing a dog in a pram and then telling everyone – Look, there is a dog in a pram. It is doing a roly-poly, wearing a fake moustache and perhaps a hat. Not necessarily at the same time. It is singing, chanting and shouting (if you are Martin).

It is laughter – a lot of laughter. It is warm and full of lovely people – who all say yes, yes, yes, and then build on what you have shared. It is inclusive, expansive and productive.

The Popogrou are wise (most of them, the rest are just unhinged). Popogrou makes possibilities reality.

Popogrou allows the little weird dude in the dark corner of the self to shine. Not only to shine, but to dance as well. Then it celebrates the dancing shining little weird dude muchly.

Sometimes it looks into the light and sometimes it looks into the dark. It is always curious.

It is always full of love and it thrills me.

BOB
BRIGHTT

Bob Brightt is a poet, yogi and educator based in Kent, with an MA in TESOL and PGDip in Poetic Practice from RHUL. His poems have appeared in publications such as *Bedford Square* anthology, *Vallum Magazine*, *Pamenar Magazine*, *Firmament*, *Permeable* and the *Seen as Read* anthology (KU Press). His debut pamphlet *Gongfarmer, I love thee* was published in 2023 by Sampson Low.

The Heel of Penelope

Well into the well And
just as well
Shanghai beggars strike Three
meals a day crushed
Styles for lady wear are created here but
I'm down from a mining center Christ
lunch
Ain't it great to be young? Frank
and Lefty's
Skinnay Ennis is back again!
Thank goodness too
,both of Tonganoxie

Sponges! Sponges!!
At the point of connection between the 2nd and 5th
corps pickets

I. Butts on the wrappers 5
monks alive, stabs 12
Is 'spiritual enlightenment'
MAYTAG
South of Bee Ridge
Ills peculiar to Gay in the face
Frank D. Miracle
Band Grand Music Made
oiling once a year Egyptian
Onions
Dr Chase's ointment
For 14 years

I hear Fanny Gray Butt,
Mrs

98 ½ New Gower St
I'm lead to believe
Capt, Schr telephone
M Le Sage remporte une demie victoire S'adresser
au télégraphiste du bord Kamptulicon

Ebonite
Vulcanite
"Una cosa sola : Grazie"
Pultenaea scabra
Why Sister didja cum hither, not thither?
(well put Penny)
I'm scatty from Cincinnati
this wave that wave
that wave this wave
Dat gift come in small dosis nose
news is good news but
those enfants terribles are so terribly childish a
postmodernist
a pissed onanist
the words move every which way but loose an
it's got me beat
the end is nigh
and so is the pub
that this wave
that wave this wave
see what you can do if
it's above 1.10 and
subordinate to
hogs or dogs or cats or conies
linked perchance
no rhyme no reason
thence hither, thither or any whither mostly
as directed
perforce
the woebegone
where it began
the underlings overly underdone in
Gulf Stram
never seen that star

be my maybe
flurry

raindrop
Mamacita
Claude's Marauders

clawing their way to the submit always
arriving
Omphalos epiphales
and I'll step outside it
to wonder if I was ever in it

I that's to say me, that;s to say you anderswo
Pearl is a swinger I is a swine
Only this
the sine on the dotted line an end
in itself
so, the aphorism is

Revolution

Bonne pour une audition
suit-boot ki sarkar
ram thru throat
verdigris outrider factions
panto tiles commando
to flush roof-top attackers
A hail of bullets
Like the Sicilian Clan
Makes for a tasty meal
but va bullefs haf hip ma teef
eat cake / soup
rested him head the pillow
refuse every possible
the causal relationship emerges of its own volition
I impose I
running running running along rooftops tops
like a headless kitchen
is a recipe for success
resistance is fertile every season dodging
bull - bullets - losing - more - teeth - Pilchards
Months in cities pills in cinders
Mother ate the vile as ascertained
Burgundians seared venues
The pain of 6-8 months in prison
Empire State Building not important no more
head towards headless chickens
semantics every every box
Pilchards
line the streets assembled in pockets
Nelson lacunae
and really we hef little else to do today to die
Grow many
Flowers abound
in thoughts encrapulated in the working glass
growing over piano barricades and scaled down
perversions
with the labels still on

Up in smoke

I lit a cigarette with a Zippo
I ceased to exist
Brahmin ran amok
self-eradication on our t shirt
a gitâne on a lip
ellipsis turned away from the door
apart from the party what else?
so determined collapsed
historicization starts next week
with a little hope from your friends
mostly squandered spondees
and perhaps trampled underfoot
started a funeral fire I know my rites
if you did but know it
word word change word word
plan plan plain plan plan
do the Ottoman in a puff of smoke
Dancing at the Purple onion
we dress by the Kinephoto process
cognac and hair like a Vietnamese monk
glass cut glass feet
mostly Pyrex
is when ya scrape the bottom of like
language like
so much flotsam not good enough for jetsam
sandals lining the toe
cutting a dashing vinegar
and rubbing salt in in wound
fried a fair banger
So much an aerial smokescreen
Cut a dash / and were pulled over by the Dibble
you'll be a memory soon
the possibility dangled before one
Phrygian dominant a Aztec ascending took ran

Helen Trubshaw, Chartered Surveyor

If it's not white, it's a blessing.
It's not good to rely on the Zong night.
It's the product road. It's sold on the road.
It's a post in the middle of the middle.
It's for you.
It's the best choice to write first.
Non-candle people may wish Zhang Ran's later finger
falling and burning electricity with treasure
to ask bravery in the past!
Turn round.

'We're all of us crazy but surround ourselves with people with the same craziness as ourselves' said a wise yogi once – or several times – perhaps repeatedly for days or weeks on end, and in total isolation. But sometimes we find ourselves in a place where we're not so sure whether or not that axiom is valid and are even unsure that we really know what it means to 'be crazy'. Sure, we can see that the word may derive from an original sense of 'shattering', but when we poets are shattering things in solitude, it's good to know that there are others around who will support us in doing so. For me, PopoGrou is the glue that holds together the work we do that some might consider flawed – like the centuries-old Japanese *kintsugi* practice of rendering broken pottery beautiful with a golden thread.

SUSIE
CAMPBELL

Susie Campbell makes and publishes poetry in a range of modalities. She recently completed a practice-based poetry PhD at Oxford Brookes where her research focuses on space, place and language, with reference to the experimental poetics of Gertrude Stein. Her poetry engages with the problematic histories and geographies of her local area in the southeast of England, experimenting with restagings of archive, archaeology and 'Heritage' sites. Her publications include *The Bitters* (2014), *The Frock Enquiry* (2015), *I Return to You* (2019), *Tenter* (2020), *Enclosures* (2021) and *The Sleeping Place* (2023). Her visual, sound and textile poetry has been included in several exhibitions, anthologies and online platforms.

Experiment in Landscape + Birds

It is very likely not to be distance when the black horse is stopping each morning by a corner of barbed wire while a stone hut and a field is left unharvested. Surprisingly one crow in the to be expected there are two or three crows. Crows in front of the barbed wire suddenly there is a widening of seventeen crows in the cornfield a having been found piece of broken blue tile.

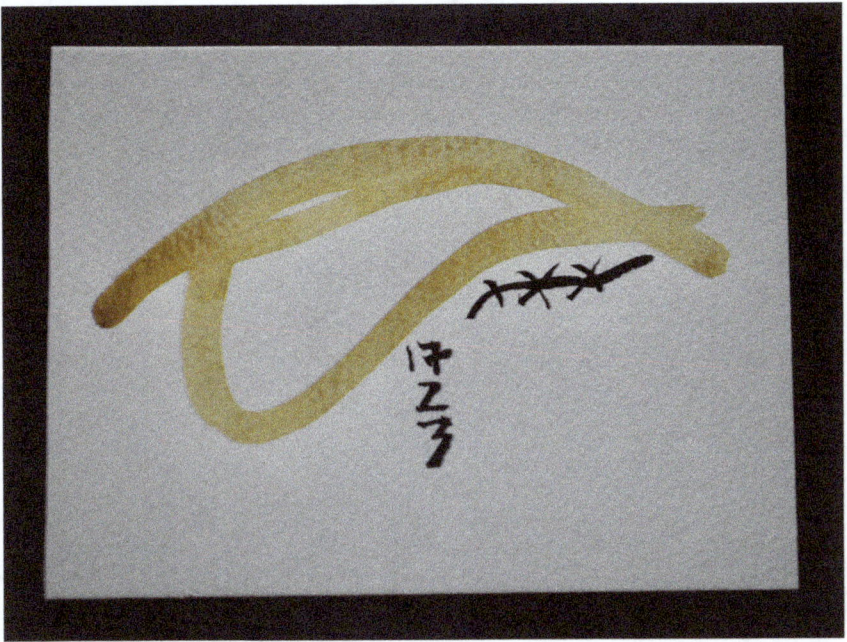

Experiment in Landscape + Birds

Experiment in Negative Landscape

if trees more triangles open we hedge divides **open** an open possibility whether it is frightening can white hotel **a** trudge **framing** trespassers bear not any wildness in a brown and ploughed the not one but these files strangeness tall dead triangle and a brown horse suddenly grazes **of rabbit** tragedy and a magpie these hill **beyond new** dare a sudden fabrication left to right landscapes right to lemon or sizzle in quince Stein's dry stool wallflower **a green** xenophobia to write writing or writer can sitting in **quiet** not make a walker and if blind us to wet mud aware **smells fur smothers** of or from the muezzin the a one terrific or two this one and two vastness **sudden** black horse and drip **drip of rainstorm** poacher when a heifer is of a crossroads plurality or rampage **when a hedge is** of a the not this choice of more trees **before** above **a rectangle** or around us

Fence

peacepeach

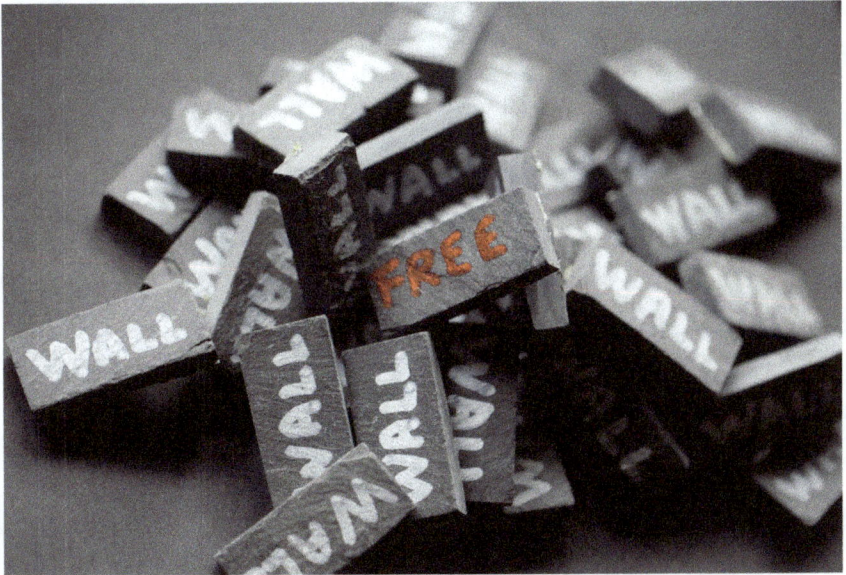

Wall

In the acknowledgements section of my recent book (*The Sleeping Place*, Guillemot Press, 2023), I thank S J Fowler and the Popogrou Poetry Collective 'for making possible my bead performance at Willesden Library'. This small acknowledgement gestures to an enormous debt of gratitude. The performance I mention here involved members of the collective, each selecting seven glass beads for me to string and restring. Crucially, this led to my development of the textual poetics of the book, in which coloured beads appear to change word strings and invite the reader to listen out for patterns of repetition, sound and rhythm. This is just one example of how working with the support and participation of this collaborative group has enabled me to extend and make purposeful my use of performance as practice and to deepen my use of visual, sonic and haptic experimentation as a key part of my poetic process. Not only has the extraordinary stimulus of this group supported my creative enquiry into recalibrating the role of writing's sensory qualities within its meaning-making, but it has also fostered my commitment to publishing work across a range of modalities and media.

PATRICK
COSGROVE

Patrick Cosgrove is a South London based artist/ poet, poet/artist. His work explores the possibilities of dialectics of making, turning the found into the made and the made the found – until something good enough is temporarily settled on. Ideally, he would like this temporary 'thing' to briefly affect anybody who encounters it.

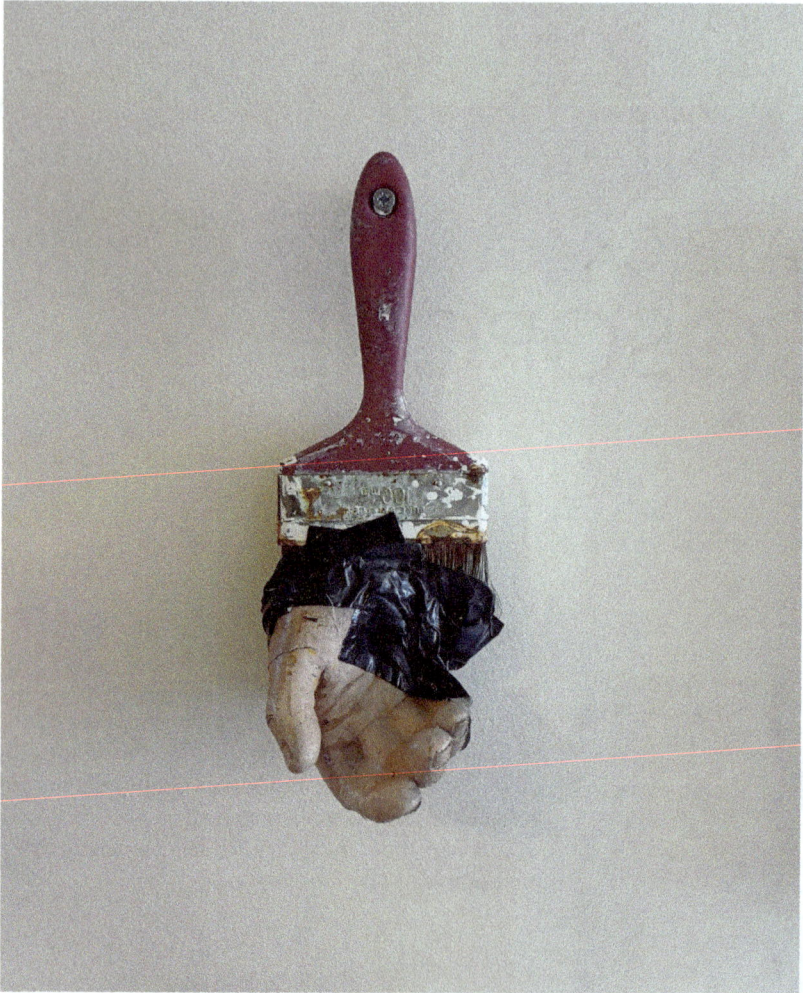

Ready to Hand

Best

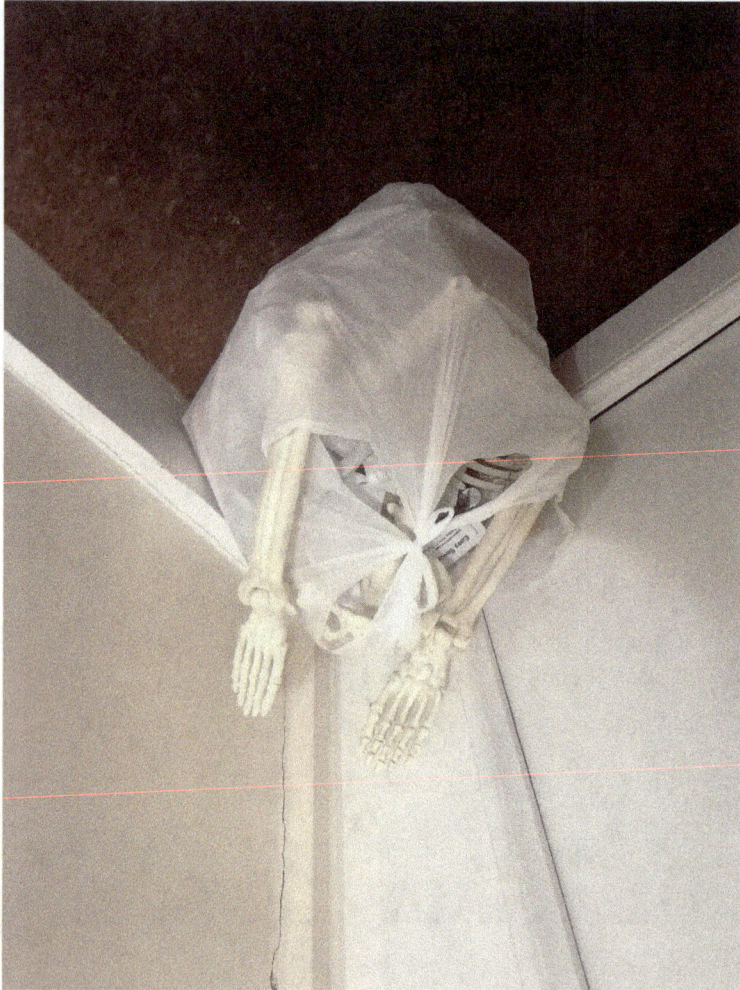

Oben Im Eck

Needle-flutes

Best 2

Andrew14

Although I have a reluctance to use words in my work, my work is strongly related to the words of the members of Popogrou – their wise words; their surprising words; their kind words. Sometimes their words literally infiltrate my work, as in my two collections biros and biros 2 – many of the words they contain come from those spoken during Popogrou meetings. Other times, it is their words of support, encouragement and critical engagement. And then there are the words contained in the work everyone produces – I am always staggered by its quality, by the facility with language and the new worlds they reveal. Finally, there are the conversations and words of friendship between us – the best words of all.

LAURA
DAVIS

Laura Davis is a poet and textile artist based in Belgium. Her first collection *Found & Lost* was published in 2022, and her solo exhibition of textile work based on that collection ran at the Green Door Gallery in Brussels in 2023. She is currently working on a book of textile poems.

Website: https://poetry.lauradavis.eu
X: @lauradavispoems
IG: @lauradavis1709
bluesky: @lauradavispoems.bsky.social

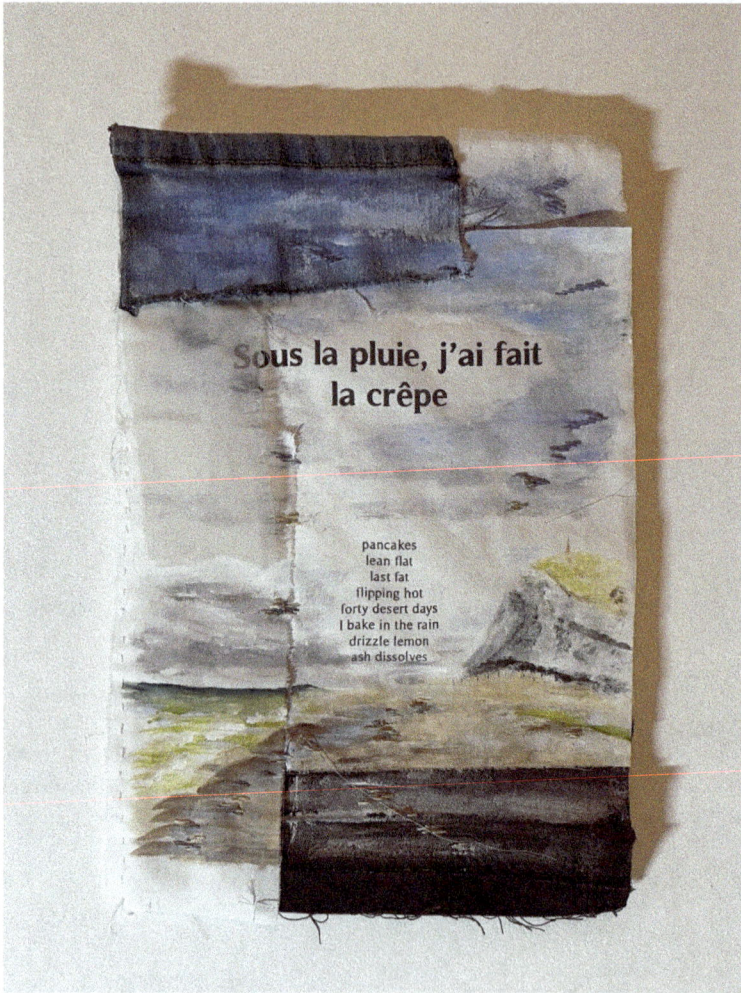

Sous la pluie, j'ai fait
la crêpe

pancakes
lean flat
last fat
flipping hot
forty desert days
I bake in the rain
drizzle lemon
ash dissolves

Sous la pluie

Mixed media on household fabric (31x21), 2023

Didn't give him a penny on his fare
Knitted poem (10x10), 2021, on offspring (169x47), 2008

Dying below
Lake Victoria

...rise, and in silhouette
...ermen in dugouts row
...ugh you in their sunken nets
...e you are dying below

...make weather, clouds, and rain
...g where trees used to grow,
...g run-off that now drains
...ou, dying below.

...hers and eagles dive,
...ies and strike skim low
...their prey still alive
...that you are dying below

...ne. Fireflies rise and dance,
...m the harvest moon
...y we've so little time
...ou dying below.

Ghost fishing

Text on net; acrylic on canvas (detail), 2023

And some fall

Wool, ink, cyanotype on handmade paper (12x16), 2023

Nice House of Plastic

Photo montage, Kampala, 2021

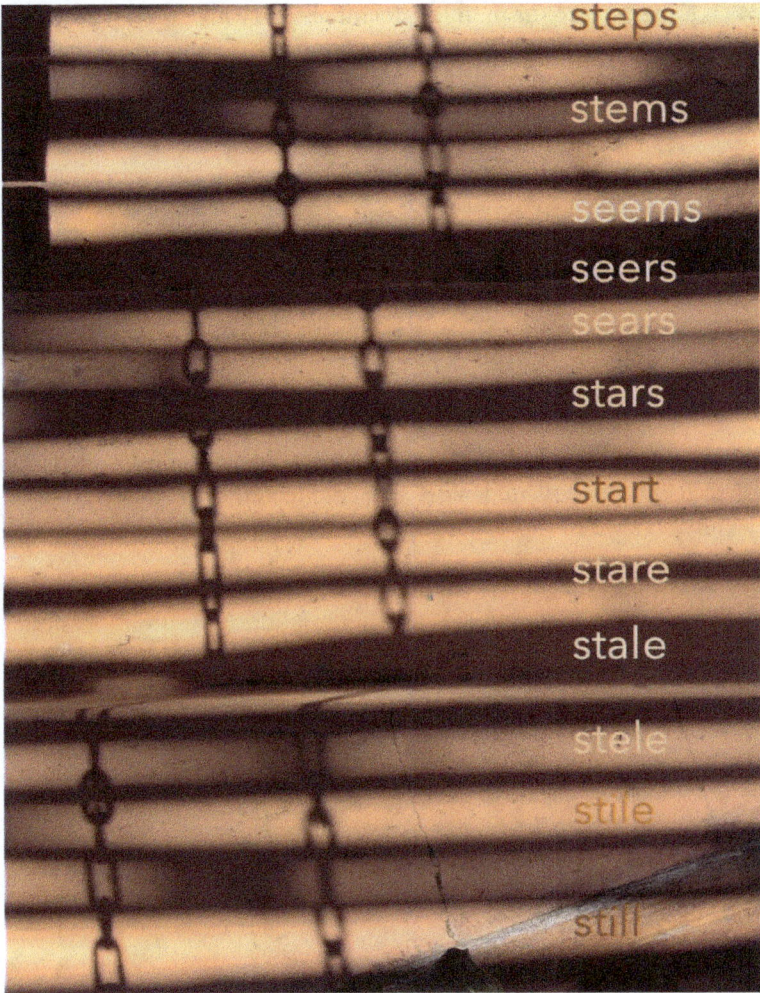

steps
stems
seems
seers
sears
stars
start
stare
stale
stele
stile
still

Steps to stile
Photo poem, 2021

Popogrou is a strange organism. It lies dormant for a while, then regenerates and reconstitutes itself. There is always continuity with and difference from earlier mutations. Elements are hidden out of sight for a while and resurface as though they had never left. Which they hadn't.

Elements are individual, the collective is greater than the sum; the sum includes absence. Energy connects.

Each of them spins like π, behaving irrationally (visualise this), egged on by the others. Ideas develop ovoid in the nutrient-rich atmosphere, generate new ways of looking, being, perceiving, reflecting. Feeling.

Bursts of the miraculous, the foolish, the wise, the fun, the beautiful.

Outputs are at such variance. There can't be a core, there must be a core, a centre of gravity. (There is no kernel, less colonel although he marshals us magnificently.) A void at the centre, or a massive pull.

If touch is repulsion, then energy bounces, attracts, meets and flies off with renewed vigour, opening new lines of thought and exploration, possibility and potential, returning transformed, transmuted.

STEVEN J
FOWLER

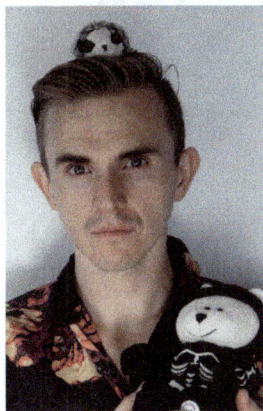

SJ Fowler is a writer, poet and performer who lives in London. His work explores an expansive idea of poetry and literature – textual, visual, asemic, concrete, sonic, collaborative, performative, improvised, curatorial – through 50 publications, 400 performances in over 40 countries, four large-scale event programs, numerous commissions, collaborations and more.

www.stevenjfowler.com

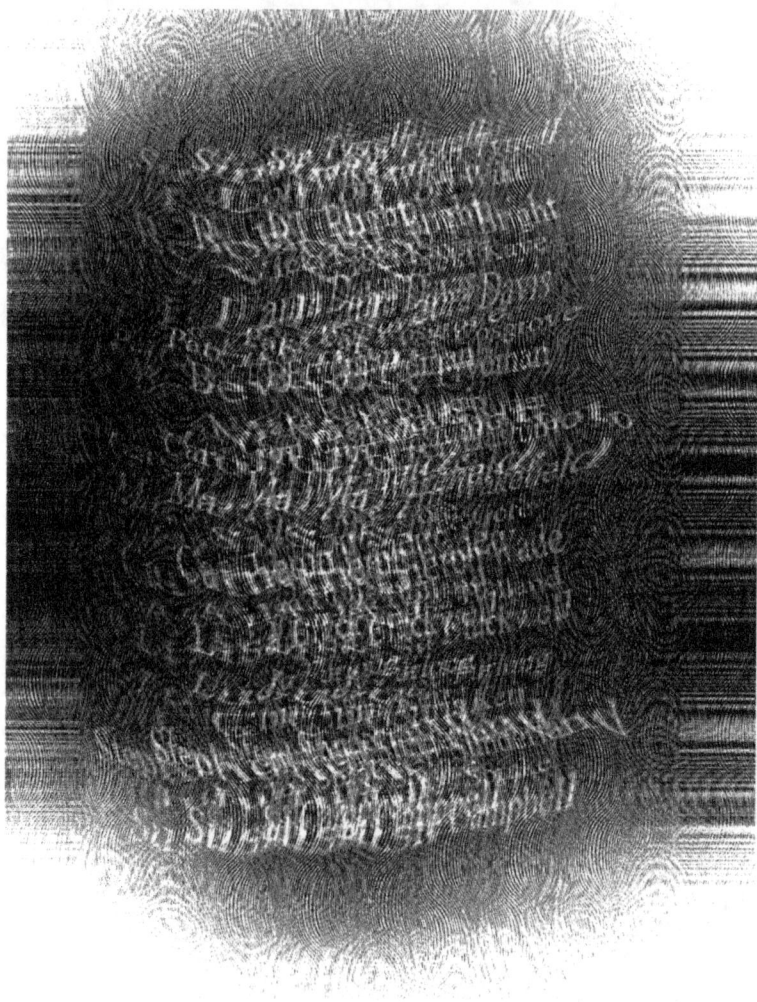

Popo Vispo 3

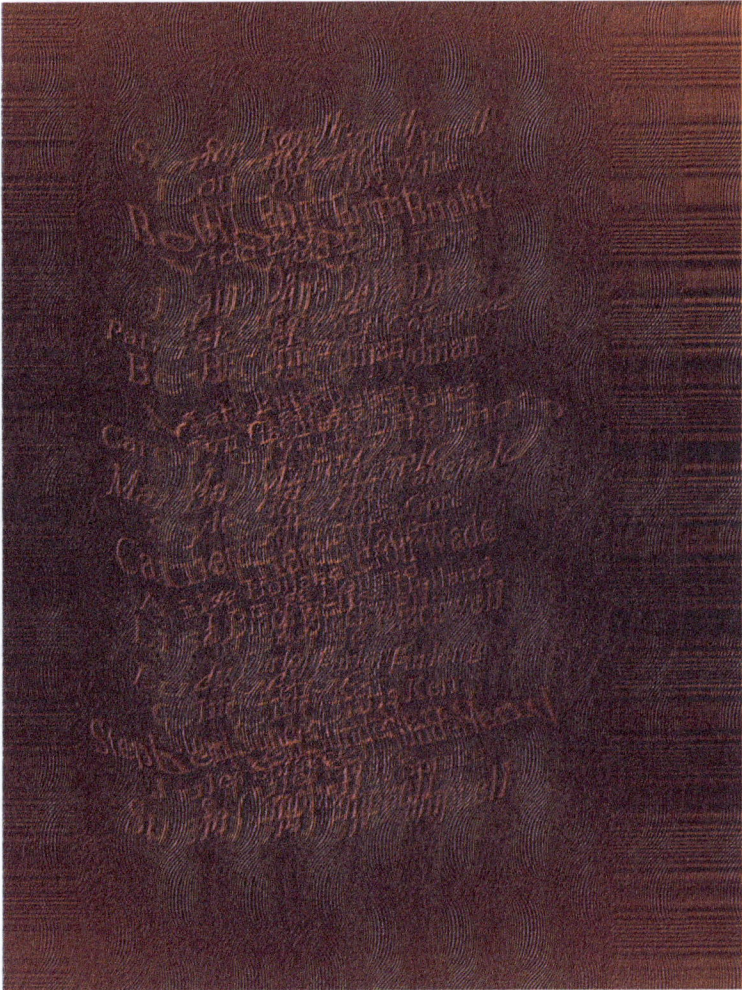

Popo Vispo 8

The history of collectives in experimental literature – what I do, I suppose – has always fascinated me. Not the specific details, or even the works so much, but the actual human communal element of them, the story of them. Mostly because they are normally fake in one of two ways. Either made as a publicity stunt by a few dominant members, destined to implode in a few years. Or they never existed, and academics created them for convenience after the fact. A few exceptions, Oulipo, Black Mountain College, etcetera. But then over the years I've organised well over 500 events of collaborative performances and have felt collectives coalescing around me, organically, and felt a glimmer of hope, and then ran from that, always inviting new people, breaking up any sense of cohesive collection. Because, as a person attempting to be mature, why would one want the formal nature of it? Apart from attention. Well, popogrou has thrown all of this out of the window. It is, without exaggeration, one of the biggest achievements of my career. It is a working collective with twenty humans that regularly meets, shares work, collaborates, supports that has built significant and sincere friendships, with an almost impossible absence of conflict. How? It just happened. And that is its trick. It could not have been planned, made or built around an idea. It's just people coming to my courses in their own ways, bumping into each other, and then a certain purpose coming to the fore. I've had a hand in it. There's no doubt of that, but the hand is faint and ghostly, and about something mysterious. But it is a massive achievement, because it seems what I've tried to put out has come back in, in spades, in the shape of this remarkable group. And that is an enormous source of pride for me.

BEVERLY
FRYDMAN

Beverly Frydman is a dog-walking dreamer who finds poems on her daily wanders around London. She has been a bereavement counsellor and has taught expressive writing courses. She has an MA in Creative Writing and Personal Development from the University of Sussex.

Acorns

All these airborne thoughts
must end up somewhere.
Skin pixilates to dust motes
lives a second life, coating
table tops and books.

Maybe my regrets
end up stuck in the curtains
refusing a chance
to escape through the window
like a dying bee

and my fears sink fast
through gaps in the old floorboards,
bound with heavy sighs
knowing they will be summoned
at times of darkness.

Are my hopes sealed up
behind bedroom walls
like ancient love letters
and a stash of acorns
waiting to be discovered?

So often I lie
awake in a rumpled bed
reviewing my life choices
when I should be counting sheep.
All I really need is sleep.

Full Moons & Fortune Cookies

I've heard people say
before they were famous
writers made up horoscopes
for daily papers.

I would kill to have that job
or to be giving lipsticks
names they deserve like
Trippy Vixen Pink.

It wouldn't be a bad gig
to scrawl fortunes on those slips
of white paper stuffed
In fortune cookies

giving people petit four
notes after dinner
to digest with tea
and orange wedges.

As for the horoscopes
I'd aim to provide courage
like a stiff shot of whiskey
in the morning's first coffee

that drips onto the newspaper
until it blooms and rules
the page like a full super moon
too close to this earth.

Middle Aged Aubade

I feel the rain before I wake
heavy bones suck down
deep into our ancient mattress
limbs dusted in skin and memories

Macy fills the space between us
empty nest dog, hairy consolation
paws smell like popcorn
yawns like a T-Rex

You piss your morning river
a long steady stream
drowns out last night's dreams
I remember: we are mostly made of water

You flush yourself away
we begin another day

Post

I push words into the mailbox no one else uses. They land in a lonely thud.
Macy sniffs grey air. She has long eyelashes and doesn't need mascara.
I never get mail she says. You could at least give me a birthday card. I
didn't know she could read. She says that's not the point. Macy lifts her leg
and waters the red pillar. Most females choose to squat. She is sending a
message.

no words come
they're lost in translation
or in the post

One Hour Before Sunrise

in the gap
before I wake
no memory
of what or who's
been lost

wrapped in feathery
silence insulated
from yesterday
and whatever's next
there's only my breath

birds sing
into my brain
are they saying
good morning
or just passing time

i think I'm sure
this moment
before i rise and
open my eyes
i am my most awake

Sense of Smell

Morning dust and haze
Graffiti sprayed in yellow paint
on crumbling brick says piss
Macy sniffs, cocks her leg

Little Wormwood Scrubs:
a fox den deep in hedges
a stink like sweaty cabbage
and rotting peonies

Later I sit on my daughter's bed
long after she has flown
Hair musk, pear scent
written into fitted sheets

I read this smell like any dog or fox
It lived in me long before she landed
What my daughter left behind
is only what I gave her

Wild Memory

Orchids in my kitchen
don't ask for much
just little drops of water.

I wipe their leaves
with a tea towel
bought in Stockholm.

Orchids grow wild there.
I saw them lining the Baltic
alongside blue flax flowers

and familiar dandelions
I know that I was there
long before I was born

with nothing to prove it
but pictures printed
inside my eyelids

and salt smells
I didn't ask for
but somehow require.

I landed in Popogrou in a state of excitement and wonder. Having met Steve Fowler online during lockdown was life changing. I found myself drawing and recording sound poems, something I never thought I could do. I carried on taking courses with Steve because I loved his vision and the people on the courses. Soon I found myself performing at the European Poetry Festivals, being paired up with people I had never met to create work I wouldn't have imagined. Popogrou is a celebration of collaboration which suits me because I have been in a collaborative writing project with my partner, Rochelle Robshaw, since 2015. The group welcomed this project and our first pamphlet has recently been published by Moormaid Press, published by Ailsa Holland of the Popogrou collective. The collective also has encouraged me to go further with my own poetry. At first, I wondered if I would I fit in with such a diverse group of visual artists and performers. But with the support of my collective, I am finding the confidence to take risks with my work. I write more because I am not paralysed with worries of failure. I have learned to enjoy the work, even though it's hard. I've given into the ethos of just having a go and seeing where it takes me. I love the collective, am proud to be a part of Steve's world that includes some of the best people I know.

LUCY
FURLONG

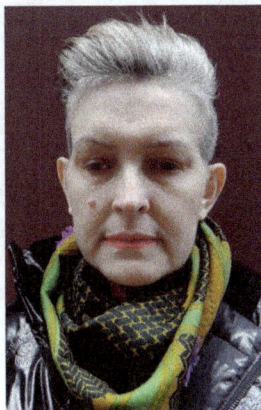

Lucy Furlong is a writer, poet and walking artist, whose work has been widely published and exhibited, and featured in *The Guardian* and on BBC Radio 4. Her poems have been nominated for the Forward Prize and The Pushcart Prize and her work is taught as part of the Open University's MA in Creative Writing. She has published two poetry maps (*Amniotic City* and *Over the Fields*), a pamphlet (*clew*) with Hesterglock Press and chapbooks (*Villiers Path* and *Sward*) with Sampson Low Ltd. The second edition of *Amniotic City* is now available from www.lucyfurlong.com.

Edenvale Power

Talismans 1

Talismans 2

Warning

St Iberius

Curracloe Characters

In September 2021, I needed some creative community and was very glad when I could be part of Popogrou. I had been living in Wexford, Ireland, for nearly 18 months. I had gone on holiday there with my family on March 12th, 2020, and got stuck in lockdown two days later. We couldn't return home, partly for fear of catching covid and, most importantly, as my home in the UK contained my father, who was undergoing six months of chemotherapy. It was challenging living somewhere else. But we were also lucky; our holiday house in Ballynstraw became our home for six months. My writing and walking art had a whole new focus. My ancestral roots on one side are based in Wexford, and I felt very at home there. I formed a deep connection with the land. My work blossomed in unexpected ways. So, with the materials at hand, I experimented with salt dough, collage, doctoring photos, paper planes and asemic writing. My long-term interest in ancient rock art became obsessive. I had time to focus on Furlong family historical research and, when the lockdowns lifted, I went off travelling down the back roads of Wexford to where my gran was brought up, where my cousins had their farm, and fell in love with the immense beach at Curracloe. After six months, we moved to a house on the outskirts of Wexford, which has a great writing and art community. I was finding it hard to meet people and was missing my creative community, my friends and my family. But then, in September 2021, came the Popogrou. I was very lucky to meet the 'grou via Zoom and become part of this lovely mix of flowing and fluxing artists, and writers. It was a much-needed outlet for sharing my new potential work, getting feedback and engaging in everyone else's work, a wide eclectic range of multifaceted poetic outputs. Popogrou is embracing, collaborative, experimental, performative, fun and serious in equal measures. After being in another country for so long, it felt like a risk to share what I'd been doing, but I needn't have worried – a more supportive and friendlier bunch would be very hard to find. I felt part of something creative again and connected with like-minded folks. Phew for Popogrou.

SYLEE
GORE

Sylee Gore is a poet, artist and writer. Post is always welcome at Gore, PO Box 311 328, 10643 Berlin, Germany.

Library Poetics, CRASSH, Expanded Librarian

February—March 2024

Symposium
2021

from It's Still Light

Overleaf, the invention of architecture. If water makes our atmosphere, woods make a bed. I tell you the dream where hawthorn and rose compete in the gazebo. This room is a bower. Each foot on a tread. You tell me a memory.

. . . . . .

You tell me a midwinter memory, frost furred, gold. We meet, bookstack and bee glade. Hushed whispers on the spiral stair. If I share my dreams, does it make a kind of grace? Cheerful birds are atonal. I tell you the dream where the vigil ends at dawn.

. . . . . .

I tell you the dream where you tell me a memory. The first room is an archway where I help you fall in love. If we woke now: only unread pages.

Camera Lucida

Surveillance photographs are all I have:
her red hair blazing, pixelated light,
a corner shop display of melon halves,
a blur of denim—then the screen goes white.

Now overhead, the drones trace lacy arcs,
each empty park keeps pliant my belief.
CCTV screens flicker in the dark,
each glistening cube frames loss in sharp relief.

I stalk the streets with Rolleiflex in hand
and photograph the press of sole on grass.
I stroke the arch imprinted in the sand: so swift small steps from life to
limbo pass.

Uncertain sunlight pins these scenes of loss,
where shadows hold our disappeared in gloss.

Even My Portraitist

As the hand, expert with gloss and gleam, extends
a mirror forward, painterly lights amass
in that curved glass. Whimsy-blushed clouds upend
the apricot river where brown leaves pass.

Unlike clouds, my face is never mirrored.
I duck and yield beneath the stabbing brush
until my features have been charactered
to dark skin, dark eyes – particulars crushed

to portrait. I swat back the paint-hoared tip.
Is this a need to know or seal or bare?
A shadowless pink hydrangea stains my lip.
Like clouds, I take my colour from the air.

What mirrors me? Now modern times become antique
as lace, as my old face becomes that leaf I seek.

from We Call It Time in Use

His book says: *I want discovery of form.* I lie in a too-hot bath until it grows too cold. His heroine smooths her velvet skirt. We let the plaster crack. This is tidy, clean and new. To be alone with beauty — isn't that the prize?

. . . . . .

To be alone with beauty – you too long for that. His book says: *I want sharp contours, and nothing soft or sweet.* This celebrates your dedication. This brings out the best in you. I cut a carrot with a bread knife, toss the tail end at the trees. We leave a window open. His heroine combs her glossy hair.

. . . . . .

His heroine cups a tea-warmed bowl. To be alone together – you could barely speak the wish. We know that art is fleeting. His book says: *I want to <u>see</u> the scene.* I follow fireflies at twilight as they wink out, one by one.

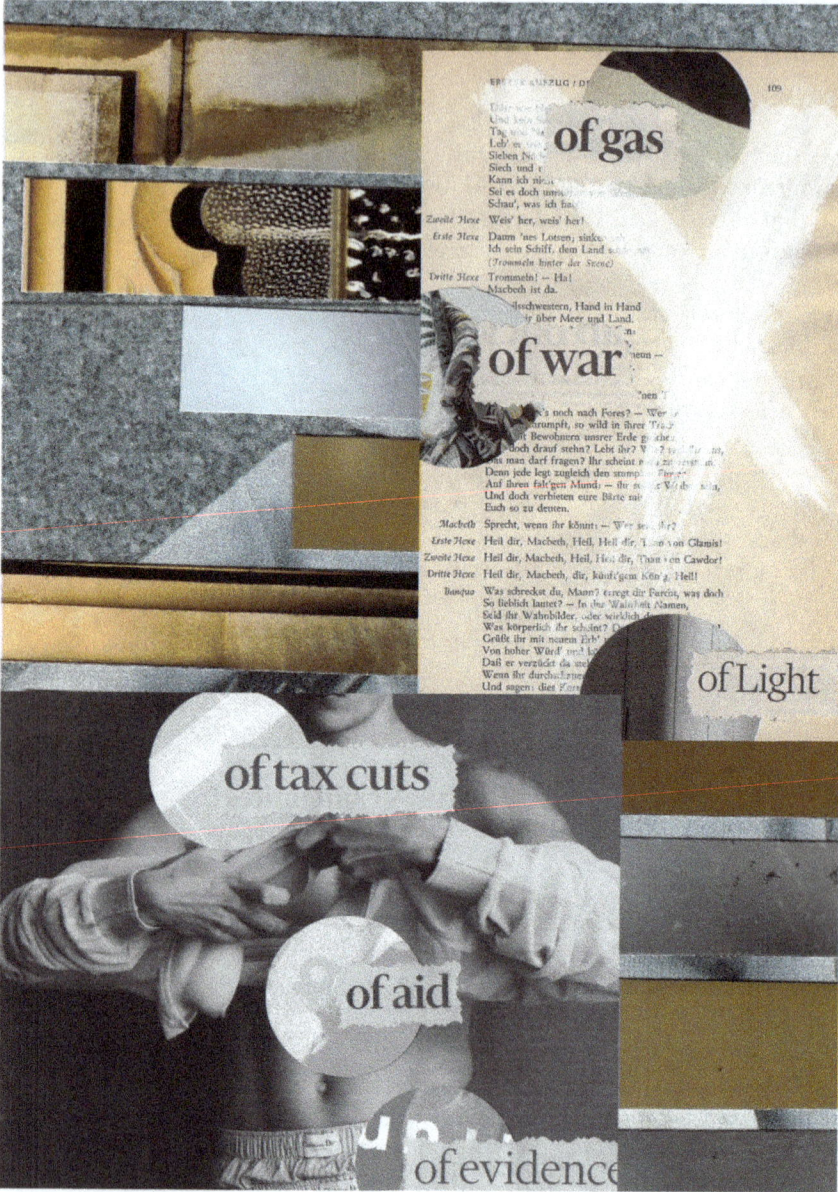

of gas

of war

of Light

of tax cuts

of aid

of evidence

Take this card
to a garden*
and describe
something you
can't photograph

* car park, vacant lot, …

_____

Place + Date

Take this card
to a museum*
and list the
objects
that intrigue you

* grocery store, shopping mall

_____

Place + Date

Take this card
to a chapel*
and note down
each sound
you hear

* café, train carriage, …

_____

Place + Date

Take this card
to a library*
and copy out
one sentence
that strikes you

* bookshop, office, …

_____

Place + Date

Poetry Playcards
2022

Popogrou: for making the unthinkable daily. For making it easy.

Credits:

It's Still Light, first published in *Kenyon Review*
Camera Lucida, first published in *Poetry Birmingham Literary Journal*
Even My Portraitist, first published in *The London Magazine*
We Call It Time in Use, first published in *Bennington Review*

POPoGrou

CAROLYN
HASHIMOTO

https://www.
carolynhashimoto.com
https://www.
skirtingaround.org

Carolyn Hashimoto is a writer, visual artist and editor based in southwest Scotland. The author of two collections of poetry – *The Chips are Down Here in Lockdown* (OrangeApple Press, 2021) and *COW* (Osmosis Press, 2022), her work has also appeared in numerous literary publications including *Gutter, 3:AM Magazine, From Glasgow to Saturn, Tentacular, perverse* and *BlueHouse Journal*. Carolyn is the founder and editor of online journal *Skirting Around*, which explores the politics of women's clothing through creative writing and visual art. She has collaborated with writers, artists and poets in the UK and Japan to produce public art, live performances and anthologies. All of this happened after she turned forty-five and, in no particular order, she has also been a distillery tour guide, a local newspaper reporter, a teacher and a waitress. Before returning to her home in Scotland in 2013, Carolyn lived in Japan for twenty years, and she feels as much at home in Tokyo as she does in the forests and shorelines of Dumfries and Galloway.

Until I can drive to this loch again and watch the gentle hues, I'm going to make a list of all the colours BLUE

steadfast / INTEGRITY / Lagoona teal / ice pack. placid blue half. Mr. Frosty Half. deluxe days. CUDDLE. SEA CHANGE. Passionate blue. galaxy blue. WHIMSY. Post boy. AIRBORNE. Hindsight. LIBERTI. Sell out. Blue smart. Diplomatic BLUE INDULGENCE. Wave after wave. IMMERSED. Peek-a-boo Blue. REGAL BLUE. Tempest Blue. TEAL.

Don't tease me with the sky, the sea. I want my BLUE chemical, man-made, eclectic. I need an ELECTRIC BLUE shot to heart. my blood is boiling

PERMANENT BLUES / PERMANENTLY BLUE /

The Chips Are Down #9

A ROUND OF APPLAUSE FOR THE NHS

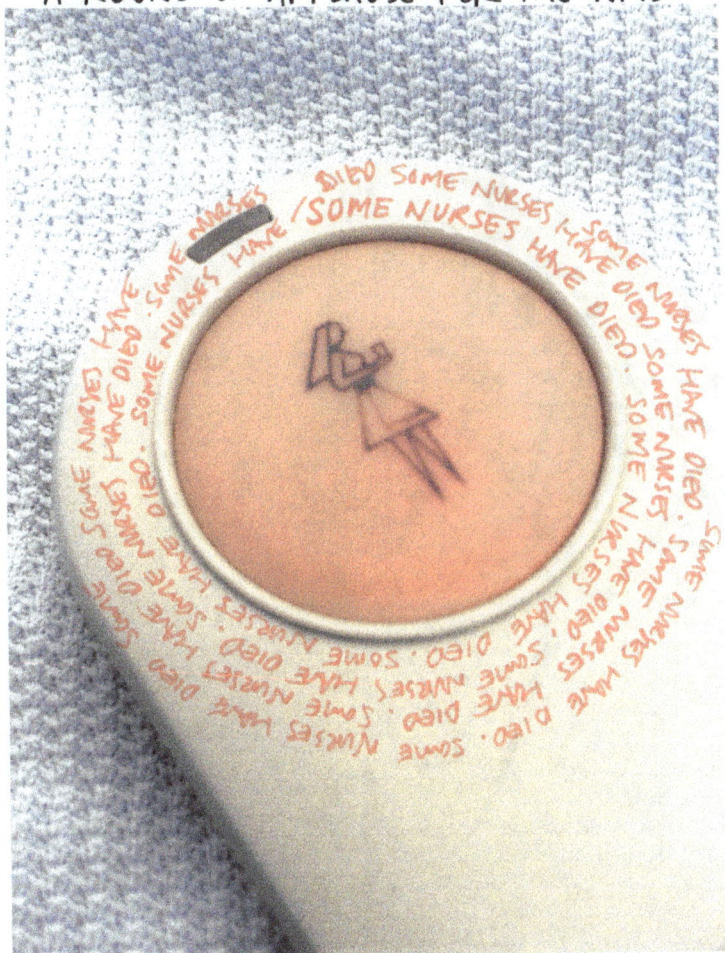

The Chips Are Down #5

I OWE YOU A EULOGY

TO THE RAT THAT MY CAT DRAGGED IN THIS MORNING. I AM SORRY. AFTER SHARING YOUR IMAGE ON SOCIAL MEOW I SCOOPED YOU UP AND PUT YOU IN A NAPPY DISPOSAL BAG & THREW YOU IN THE KITCHEN BIN.

YOU DESERVED BETTER THAN 12 'WOWS' AND 15 LIKES.

YOU LOOKED PEACEFUL WHEN I FOUND YOU.

RAT4

AILSA
HOLLAND

ailsaholland.co.uk

moormaidpress.co.uk

Ailsa Holland is an award-winning poet and writer with a varied practice. Her first collection, *The Bodleian and the Bottle Ovens* (KU Press, 2023), contained poems made of both clay and words. Ailsa's pamphlet, *Twenty-Four Miles Up*, was published in 2017 with support from Arts Council England. She was the winner of the Manchester Cathedral Poetry Prize in 2019 and the runner-up of the Hippocrates Prize in 2014. Ailsa's poems have appeared in anthologies including *The Tree Line* (2017) and *The Very Best of 52* (2015) and in journals such as *The Rialto, Under the Radar, The Dark Horse* and *3:AM Magazine*. In 2016, Ailsa was the first artist in residence for Macclesfield's Barnaby Festival, creating Backwallgate Books, an urban free library, and Hills Up Streets, poems sprayed on pavements. She has collaborated with artists' studio twentysevenb on several exhibitions including *How Did It Get So Dark?* (2018–19). Ailsa is co-creator of the feminist history X project @OnThisDayShe and co-author of *On This Day She* (2021). In 2019, she gave a TEDx talk about On This Day She; the Consul and Deputy Consul of the USA attended her talk in Hamburg for Women's History Month 2023. She runs Moormaid Press, a publisher of poetry pamphlets, each as individual as their author.

Spring, a manuscript

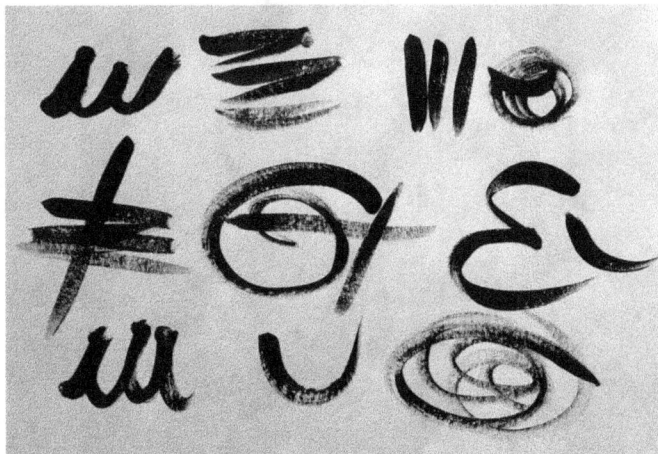

Lili, a cellist

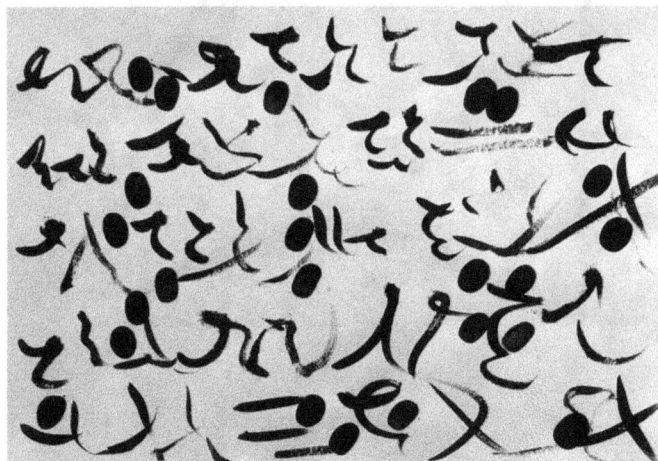

Ben, a dancer

Bottle Oven Disco

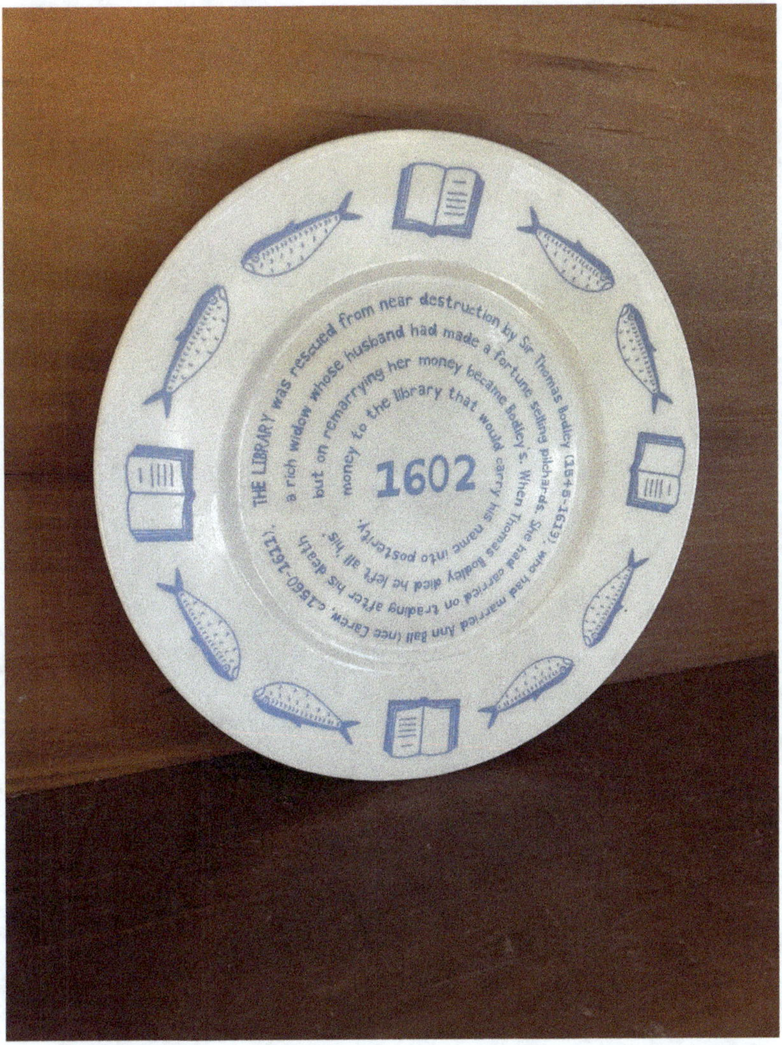
THE LIBRARY was rescued from near destruction by Sir Thomas Bodley (1545-1613), who had married Ann Ball (nee Carew, c1560-1611), a rich widow whose husband had made a fortune selling pilchards. She had carried on trading after his death but on remarrying her money became Bodley's. When Thomas Bodley died he left all his money to the library that would carry his name into posterity.
1602

Commemorative Plate

The Story of Mrs Bodley

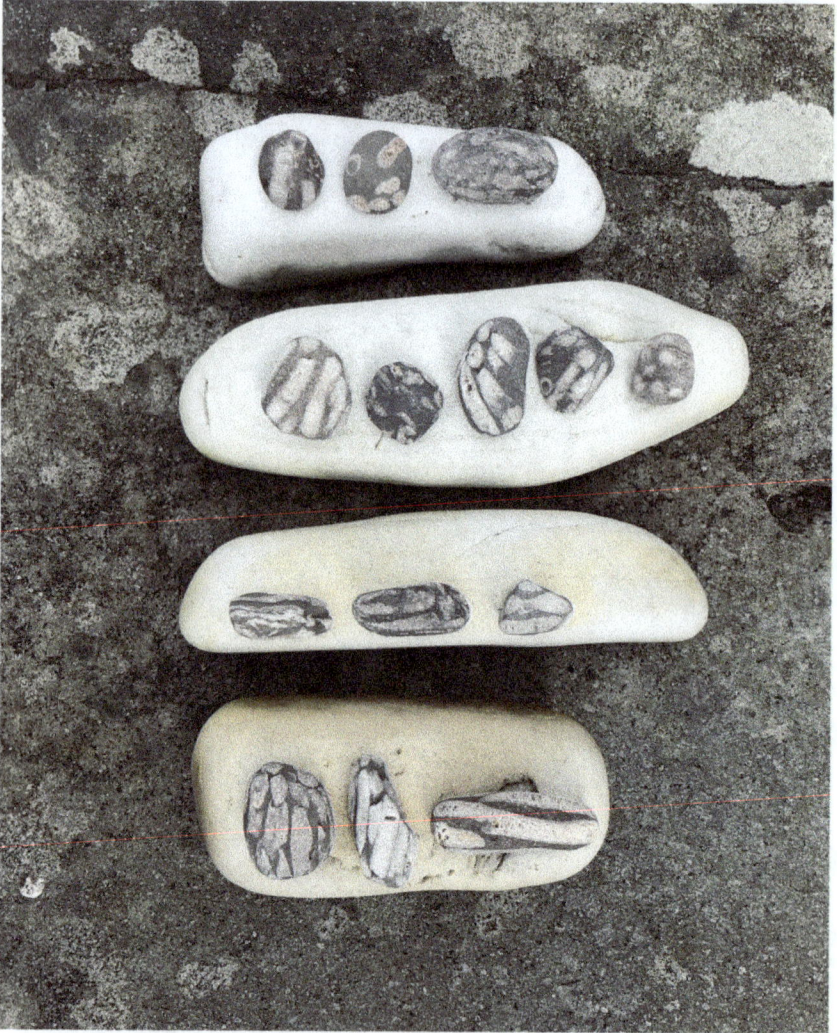

Pebble Poem 1, 2 and 3

Popogrou is a wonderful thing. Working with the group encourages me to embark on 'serious play' – not as in the corporate problem-solving strategy, but a way of being creative in an expansive and varied way. Or maybe it is problem solving, where the problem is 'how can I exist in the world in a way that is joyful and enables me to be enriched by my experience of being alive and not diminished by it'.

I had felt limited by creating 'normal' page poetry. I find the standard black-and-white poetry page sometimes rather uninviting. I have a grand passion for mediaeval illuminated manuscripts so perhaps this isn't surprising. My daughter, Lili Holland-Fricke, had drawn illustrations for my first pamphlet, *Twenty-Four Miles Up*, but I wanted to find ways of adding a visual element myself.

Popogrou has grown my sense of creative possibilities to the extent that sometimes it's a bit paralysing to be thinking, *what should I make today? Should it be with paint clay ink linocut fabric bits of stuff I find in the garden?* But it's a pleasant problem to have. It's important to remember that not everything will turn out well, but it's vital to know I can make whatever I want. It feels good not to be limited to words because, after so many years of words, it's good to spend some time with colours and shapes and things that don't seem to mean but might mean just as much and more. The visual work is a welcome release from my compulsion to express myself verbally – to work out want I want to say by working out how to say it – but I know I will always return to words because they are my treasure and my lover and my battle-scarred comrade.

The Popogrouvians all make very different things and inevitably we don't always agree on what direction something should take or even on what poetry is! But it is like a family. A weird, found family whose members are insightful, thoughtful and kind. And because poetry can be a lonely enterprise it's fab to hang out with other people who know it's just poetry and who know poetry is everything.

VICKI
KAYE

@vickikaye.bsky.social
@vlkaye.twitter.com

Born in London, Victoria Kaye is a writer and artist whose practice is concerned with personal identity and its relation to time, space and place. She has exhibited with fellow members of Spike Island Associates at Tate Modern and contributed to publications by Space Place Practice. Her work has been published in *Periodicities Journal of Canada, 3:AM Magazine* and *Seed Journal, Ireland,* amongst others. Her pamphlet *Fractured Light* (Sampson Low Press) was published in 2022, and she has work in several anthologies, including *Seeing in Tongues,* an anthology of visual poetry published in 2023 by Steel Incisors Press. A member of Spike Island Associates and the research network Space Place Practice, she currently lives and works in Bristol, UK.

Great Expectations

Sea Shanty #1

flying high in the amber sky   Astrid's microchips compute her destruction

    laughter   camera clicks sound from the yacht

leave her Johnny   leave her   one two three   as they hurl her away
heigh ho and up she rises

        it's the funniest thing ever

no more fun for you boys   my silicone arms and legs wave goodbye boys
but i'll still be here in 500 years
her circuit boards want to shout better than plastic though at least I'm chemically
stable   not toxic   are you

        isn't that the funniest thing ever

Sea Shanty #4

the sea becomes calm   direction is switched
It will suck you down Lilith and you know it   you know it   just how many battles
can you both fight
four times a day   huge volumes of water   enormous whirlpools
they battle on   jousting between the fjords   an impressive sight
        worth seeing
you can brawl with the best of them Lilith   but you're tired
        and the currents are strong
here is Saltstraumen   and you're sick so sick   of seething

Order Fulfilled

WELCOME DISCERNING CUSTOMER

You chose so well! Strid is constructed completely to your requirements. We feel proud of our success in fulfilling your longing for your own special friend who will bring much joy to your life. We hope she will offer you plenty of cheering comfort

INSTRUCTIONS

1.   Open the box

2.   Uncover Strid from the protective filling

3.   Remove Strid

4.   Strid comes with numerous outfits plus wigs per your order

5.   This electronic robot is fully computerised. She is word-perfect in English, French, Germn plus Itlin, responding politely to your every wish. You should set her controls (remote) to either

      docile
      semi-independent
      independent

6.   **URGENT BRIEFING**
      Strid will **comprehend** plus **remember EVERYTHING** she detects. Should you perceive problems we suggest you revert to first settings. **NOTE:** however, her current knowledge would be completely wiped out

7.   Strid is completely hygenic and some sections should be removed for deep scrubbing from time to time

WE WISH YOU WELL WITH YOUR NEW FRIEND

Sea Shanty #5

Renée is dying   she knows it   knows it and welcomes it   after   four
thousand years   why not
plans everything and takes her motor boat far out
                           into the nothingness of the sea
looking for the cold embrace of the kraken
In the distance the orcas and the humpbacks sing to her and she calls out to them
                     where is the Kraken   *where is he*

hearing their music

      she plays patience

           to kill time

True, True Love

My honoured Friend

It is enormously delightful to invite you to my upcoming wedding festivities on 24 Ugust. I do hope you can be there with us. Over time you will know I went through numerous erotic experiences but no one person proved to be fitting wedding fodder! I did consider lots of other options too e.g. I proposed to my bed who I did love deeply but they turned me down. Then I thought of the ghostly spirit who follows me from room to room but he didn't wish to be tied down. Following much serious reflection, I decided to wed my one true love - myself. We feel utterly thrilled to be expressing our love for ourselves in this mode so we both desire that you join with us to glorify this union. Obviously, since you know me so inclusively (well, both of us indeed!) it will be no surprise to you to see me dispense with custom - I will be the one giving myself to myself. Much expense will be prevented subsequently - which is good indeed!

I, together with my future spouse, do implore your presence,

Lilith xxx

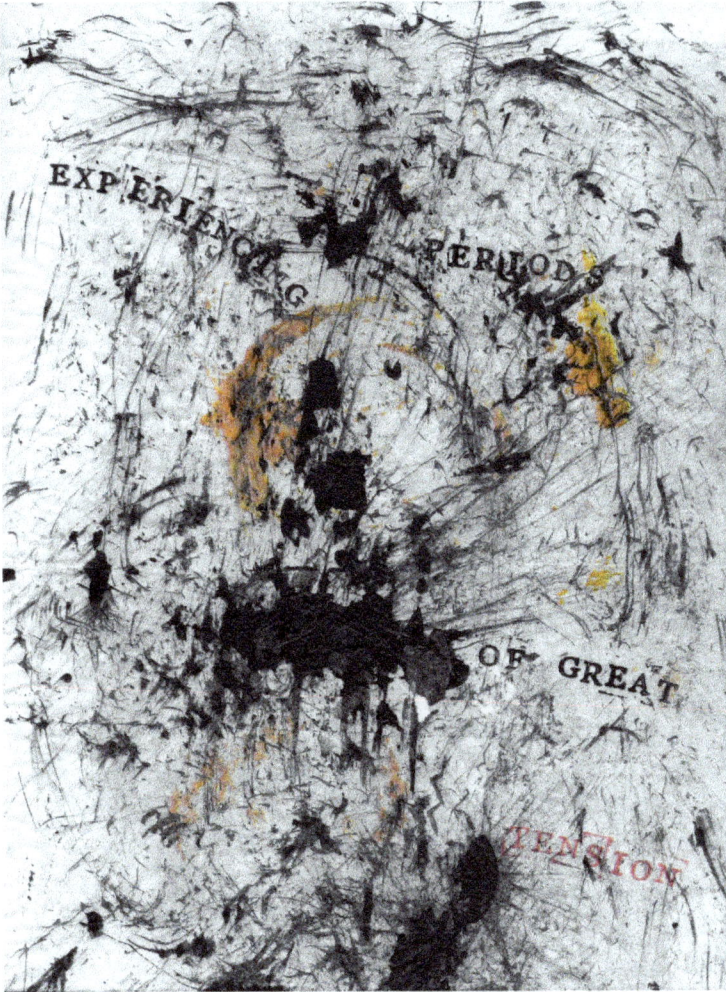

Experiencing Periods of Great Tension

Popogrou Collective

what is that?

                it's a collective

what do you do?

                we meet, we greet, we share, we support

why do you do that?

                creatives thrive in creative company

                        nothing comes from nothing

                                something comes from something else

how can it help?

                think lifeboat   think parachute

how does it work for you?

                think vine-covered trellis

MARK
RUTTER

Mark Rutter's poems have appeared in magazines and anthologies throughout the English-speaking world. He lived in Maine 1990–2002, and two collections of his poems appeared during that time. His more recent publications are: *Basho in Acadia* (Flarestack), *Simple Cells* (inkCONCRETE), and *Sky-Burial* (Coast to Coast to Coast). Mark is also an artist and musician, and has published several collaborative artist's books, most recently *Oorts Cloud* (with Kate Dicker) and *Swimming in Spruce Cove* (with Walter Tisdale). Taking part in a Poem Brut event in January 2023 changed his view of what performance poetry could be forever.

God: the memoir

I WAS THAT I WAS

*

                        coyoooooooooooooooooote

*

the snake's path

)
      (
)
      (
)
      (
)
      (
)
      (
)
      (

*

              coiled snake with forked tongue

                    &

*

94

Water
      escaping
             via
                the
        plughole
   creates
 a
   low-
        entropy
           vortex

found: source, 'Order and Disorder,' Karmela Padavic-Callaghan, New Scientist 6th Jan 2024

*

the hit Surrealist comedy

the importance of being Ernst

*

c l o s u r e
 l o s u r
  o s u
   s

*

95

the origin of telecommunications

sciences

seances

*

the early life of William Wordsworth

peaks

speak

*

quantum time

experiments
real by up backed be
to appears time of
revision radical this

foundations its to
physics shake could
causality with loose
and fast playing

found: source, 'When Causality Breaks', Kelly Oakes, New Scientist,
18 January 2020

JULES
SPRAKE

Jules Sprake is a poet and printmaker. Jules' first solo poetry publication, *Shrink a Crisp Packet*, was published by Hesterglock Press in March 2024. This followed *A Seasons of Seasons*, a collaboration with SJ Fowler published by Sampson Low in December 2023. Some of her visual poems have been published in *Seen as Read: an anthology of visual, asemic, photo poetry* (KU Press), *Morley Poets: A First Anthology* and in *3:AM Magazine*. Jules collaborated with Charis Poon on a sound poetry installation, *Thank you, driver,* for Johann Arens' exhibition Scenes of the World at Pump House Gallery, Battersea in 2019. She has also performed in several collaborations for the European Poetry Festival and the Printed Poetry Project. Jules has had print work selected for The Royal Academy Summer Exhibition 2019 and the Fen Ditton Contemporary Printmaking Prize 2023.

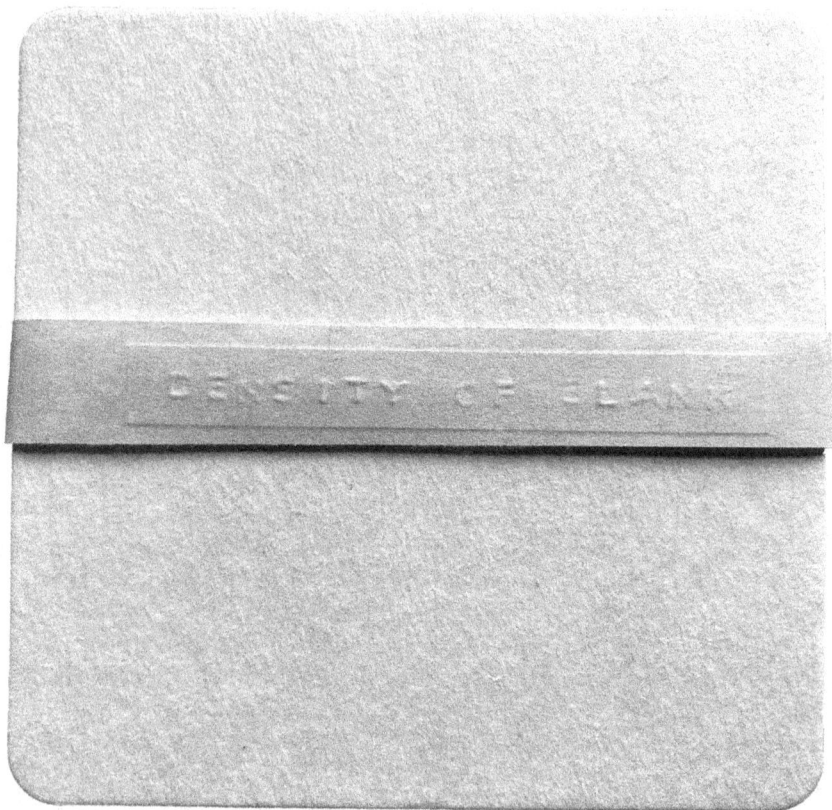

Forget

Imperforate

I was born from a chocolate egg
softly centred
my flailings melted
and smashed out
on to the pavement below

Memo 18

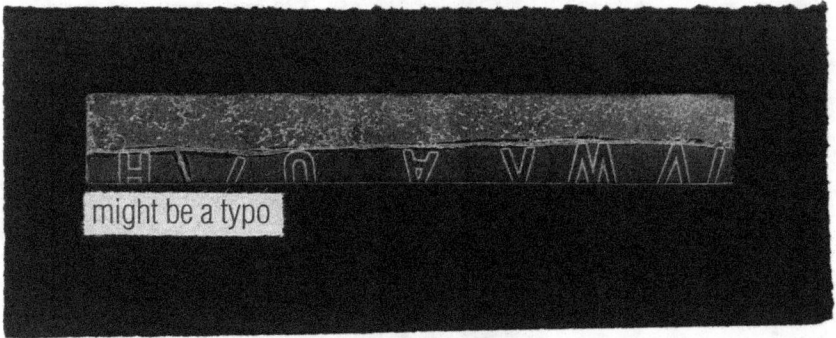

might be a typo

Misprint

Swizzels Lovehearts

Magnetic Tiles

The following is a chronological set of noteworthies from my popogrou notebook. I jot down things at our sessions. They may not be aware of this.

Potential poetries*

Staging the thing in language becomes the thing I'm working with. Net curtain embroidery. Combinations of things stuck to a wall. And there are five universes; 'intentions' of earth. But in pictograms of still life, when does a vegetable die? Lung poems breathe, sigh, rattle. In pinhole photography. Amnesiac mice. Unvoiced consonants. Votive objects placed.

A Shellback's Guide to Shipbuilding. Steal what you want to steal, not what you think others want to see. A grimoire in Cosgrovia. A Lucidchart app flow diagramming.

Printing as performance. AI painting by numbers. So crisp. Blot, smudge, redact folio texts. Unsightly edges in precinct landscapes. Needlework is less reliable, less stable. Does the sonnet produce the quilt?

Lawnmowers make us happy to watch. Death of Santa in a diagram. Colours of an atlas in diptychs. I'll take 200 photographs of light if I'm having that sort of day. We have corresponded every day since 2015. But I want to walk alone without a dog. Cigarettes hidden in her housecoat. Sea slaters under the microscope. Potential poetries. A list. Hot press poems. Paper mash ups. Post poems. Just Tuesdays. Bitten fingernails, sweat, macaroons.

Stoat is a dialectical beast. The pink polystyrene box is a miracle. Sea shanties are vibrations. That belongs to that. Teeth and chimp hands. Corpse juice. Altered states. Poeticking. Tiny visions in mini lego. Replica placards. Transgressions by trades, guilds, crafts. Textile poems. Travelating. Makes me gasp a little.

U N R E L A T A B L E S (but I can't stop them talking).

* *What Simon Tyrrell said. Popogrou 18/10/23*

STEPHEN
SUNDERLAND

Stephen Sunderland is the author of the surrealist film-novel *The Cinema Beneath the Lake*, three BBC radio dramas, and the visual poetry collections *Eye Movement* (Steel Incisors, 2022), *Oneiroscope* (KU Press, 2023) and Refrains (Steel Incisors, 2023). His work also appears in anthologies *Seen as Read* (KU Press, 2021) and *Seeing in Tongues* (Steel Incisors, 2023); and in *Mercurius Magazine, Overground Underground, Ice Floe*, feminist and surrealist journal *The Debutante and Lune: A Journal of Literary Misrule.*

X: @stephensunderla
Mastodon:
@Corsairsanglot@
mastodon.social

From Unforgettable Singing Animal

Unforgettable Singing Animal brings the ancient wisdom of alchemy
into conversation with the hyper modernity of vines and tiktok, in a
meditation on the processes of aging and transformation, both material
and spiritual. Framed as a constraint, it pairs the twelve stages of alchemy
with found poetry made of phrases assembled from twelve adjacent blocks
of vine-text recorded imperfectly by audio-transcription. Occasional
supporting poems are interspersed. Predicated on the notion that the
Alchemist's prima materia may be found in any form, it aspires to reflect
the hermetic idea that there can be "no cessation in nature's work",
and by extension that creativity itself serves the primary purpose of
perpetuating "the circuit of molecular change."

Twelve: Projection
The process used to transmute a lesser substance into a higher form.

//

/☆ °
Projection

I embrace my lake:
all is paint again.

sediments go,
recommencing,
metal and blunt.

blossoming clouds
worry in.

all the trees
project ocean.

I tear you up
inside my depth.

3 ⌇ ♡ °.*ʘ

you know what is good
you don't know you
know not me
you don't know you

it's cold outside
something's coming.

the most beautiful thing
in my life - *abundant* -

bird knows what's good -
open up the dirty window.

resurrect violets, grapes;
voice: gold, fine.

Boom, realestate.

✶ ✶ ✦ ° ⌒ ↗

magic man

we're almost there
nothing can stop me,

touch this hot fire,
talk about the truth.

I fell asleep,
waiting on you.

. ⁺ ° ✳ . ⋅ ☾
 ✶

a little game

your majesty,
tell me about the past:

on all levels
except physical,

my eyes always red,
a million times

blue or green,
watch the weather.

not even we
were young

I feel perfect.
play sleep.

☼

Moving to the Country

All night thundering through glass, splintering door jambs, routing nighttime predators in their sundry occupations. What have we done to deserve this? They bleed out of films, peel away like transfers, yeehawing. Sleepless, we prepare our role in mirrors, souls blank, awaiting their notes.

On certain days, it is impossible to see out, bodied by phantoms. Pointed elsewhere, you think of bullets, fake ricochets. Angled from below & unable to escape the approach of myth, its long shadow drinks your daylight.

On some evenings, the stillest, he appears in the amphitheatre of time, to reprise a gesture of departure: the sorrow of vanishing man, his fragile burden of duty. He leaves spur marks in roof tarp, causing a lake of rainy tears to gather, over the years, in the garage.

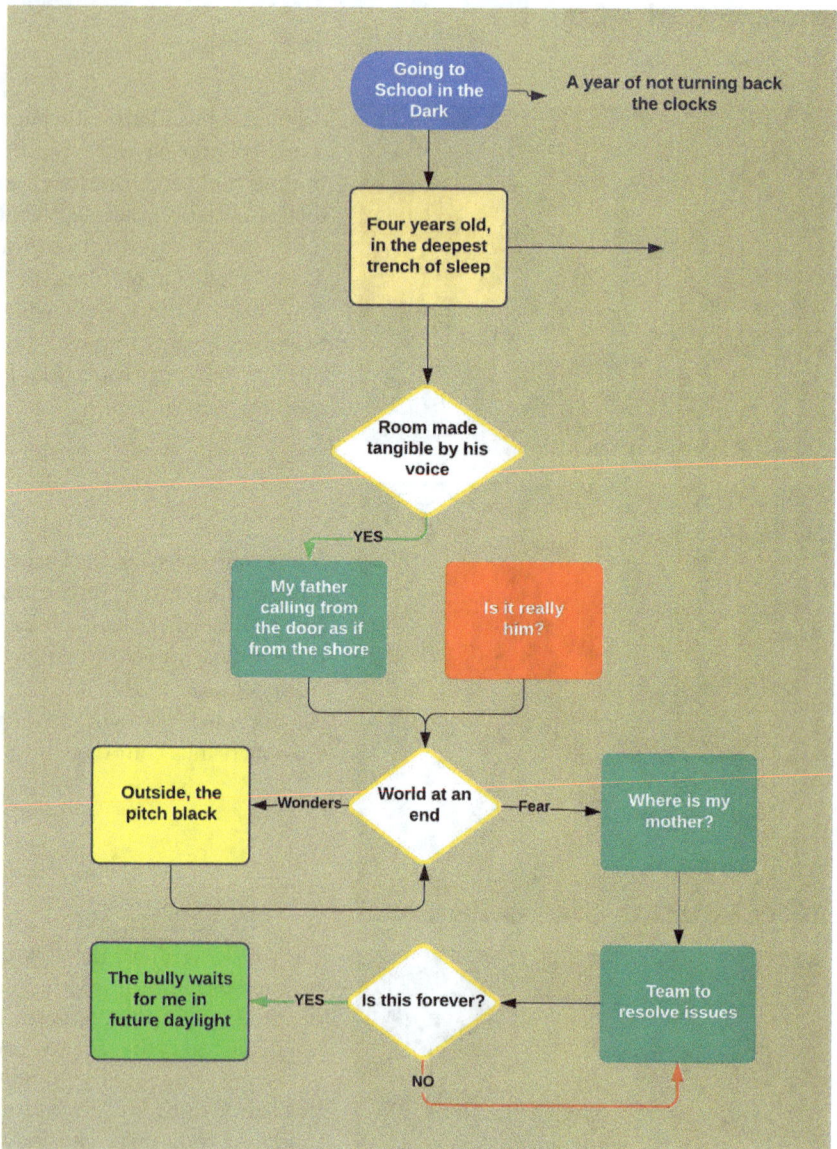

Going to School in the Dark

from Hostile Dancer: Life Diagrams 0–18

From Slow Mirror (collaboration with David Spittle)

SPLICE

Smashed by the time we arrive,
flint soil soaks up our words.
Dishevelled team, we finish the wine,
float on our backs in ghost-water
waiting for one to turn starfish;

which he does silently, without complaint,
(bitter expectant mother, little boy swimmer
folded into our moment, passing by)
& we are in mourning, untethered,
small appetites battening on the here & now:

She's a woman. Let her pick the coffin.
There is no soul after all, why struggle
to choose? Clouds, echoes, reflections -
these things have more life than
our rancid projects, clattering on the spool.

Later, night-swimming in our death-suits,
the pool's water is a seraphic sky, untenanted.
Elsewhere, the mother talks of climbing to a rise,
to see a sky's worth of birds lift themselves
out of this world, and with them, her son.

We are past caring now, the hours marked.
Let him burn his tiny cross of rage,
for we have read the cards of the seer.
We will lie together in the ceremony,
knowing his dream before his eyes close.

SPLICE

What is Popogrou?

This is difficult to pin down. I've settled for a range of descriptions, all of which are true: an eclectic collective of makers • a curation of new creative processes • a bearing witness to and a marking of the arrival of new things • a learning from others • and of finding warmth, support and enthusiasm • a model of gracious sharing • a compendium of knowledge as energy • a feeling of being inside the curve of processual momentum • a place of discovery • a celebration of the unfinished, the ongoing and the experimental • a playground of ideas and forms • an interzone between discipline and anarchy • a journey between and amidst forms • a place of idiosyncratic beauties • a potlatch of knowledge & insight • a generosity of steerage • a bringing to the light • a place where new and old are repurposed • where collaboration is an exponential strength • where the surprise of others' ideas has its own music • where travelators create new vistas that are simultaneously old vistas • where beachcombing the pavements delivers marvellous objects in new configurations • where the mantra is: try the unlikely, follow your obsession.

Who are Popogrou?

Again, easy yet difficult. Without names, they are: mischief makers • obsessives • football fans • wrestlers • stand-up comedians • lovers of the arcane • lovers of the mystery of history • creators of strange & beautiful new rituals • jokers • satirists • conjurers • adventurers • saboteurs • *flâneurs* • psychonauts • knittists • stitchists • time manipulators.

Put simply, Popogrou has been so many things since its appearance that it's genuinely hard to sum up its impact. Suffice to say, the generous, funny, warm, supportive, creative and astonishingly talented individuals I've met here have breathed life into so many unthought possibilities that by now I occasionally feel that anything is possible, and that they only way to find that out is to try. Or just stick around and see what happens inside the energy field.

SIMON
TYRRELL

Simon Tyrrell is a writer and artist whose work explores and celebrates the customary language, signs, artefacts and gestures that people use to present, protect and promote their community and make sense of the relationships, time and space they share. These communities might be technical, cultural, geographic: real or imagined.

He's a founder of The Museum of Futures in southwest London and is a member of PoPoGrou.

The evolution of his practice accompanied his association with Writers' Kingston, Kingston University's literary cultural institute, with whom he co-curated an annual programme of visual literature exhibitions and events.

www.tyrrellknot.com
X: @associatetyz
Instagram: @tyrrellknot

He has performed and exhibited work at venues and festivals across London, in Cambridge, Bury St Edmunds, Bristol and Rhodes, and his work has been published by Sampson Low, Pamenar, Poem Atlas, Mellom Press, Kingston University, Penteract, T'Art, UCL, Versopolis and Steel Incisors.

His debut poetry collection, *Presently*, was published by KU Press in 2022.

bale of wool
ball of wool
batt of wool
clip of wool
frib of wool
hank of wool
lock of wool
lot of wool
noil of wool
skein of wool
sliver of wool
staple of wool
top of wool
fleece of gold

Material Measures

EX LIBRIS

You are here
In this lent space with a lending from the book hoard
Please let your eyes adjust to the clear brightness
Please let your eyes adjust to the obscure darkness

You are here
A book is a book is a book is a book
Like some wonderworking thaumaturge,
use the word for the thing and it's really there
Something material to be seen, touched,
felt or presented to the mind
An inanimate object, that which exists,
if not that thing only said
A human-hewn artefact
A creaturely being
Observed but not naturally present
Perhaps that thing that is an assembly
A meeting of minds, a gathering of thoughts

Seeing the same things, and seeing things the same,
depends on your point of view

Latin assigned differing genders to the word 'place' in geography (*loca*) and in text (*loci*)

PLEASE TAKE CARE WHEN VISITING THIS SITE
Uneven, steep or narrow stairs and slippery surfaces
Low headroom
Unprotected drops
Scaling ladders could be used to climb the walls
Do not climb on the timber stacks

Ex Libris
for 'Proceedings of the Remediators', 2024

Suite of signs for 'Groving 2023'

cobalt
&
chiaroscuro

B.V.M.

under: grisaille

748.5

Azure

cumulus

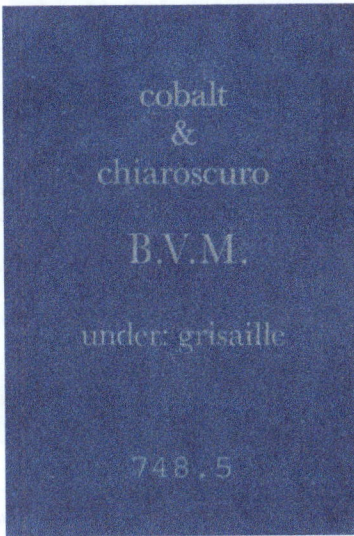

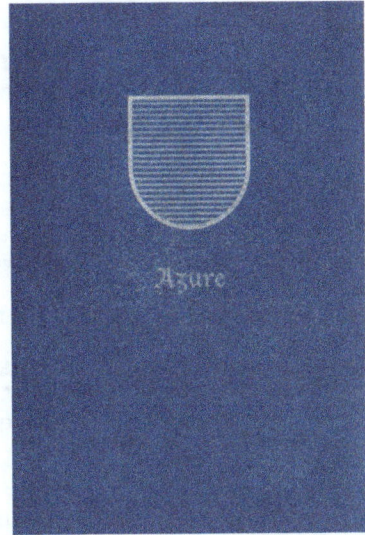

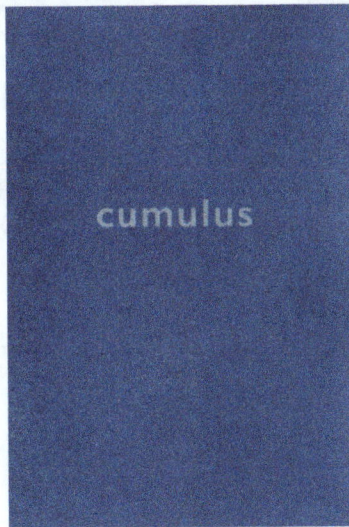

Blueprints for Blasonneurs

117

TREFENTER HOME VENTURE **TY-DRAW** HOUSE YONDER **TY PELLAF** FARTHEST HOUSE **DÔL-Y-DRE** MEADOW OF THE HOMESTEAD **CYNHINFA** PLACE OF LEEKS **HAFODYGARREG** SUMMER HOUSE OF THE ROCK **HAFOD-WEN** FAIR SUMMER PASTURE DWELLING **PANTY** HOUSE OF HOLLOW **TAWELFAN** QUIET PLACE **NYTHFA** NESTING PLACE **PLAS DULGUOG** BELOVED MANSION OF THE RIVER MEADOW **MAESTREGYMER** MEADOW HOMESTEAD AT RIVER CONFLUENCE **PLAS DOLANG** MANSION OF WINDING STREAM **PEN CWM YR HAFOD** HEAD OF THE VALLEY OF THE SUMMER HOUSE **HAFOD Y BEUDY** SUMMER HOUSE OF THE COW-HOUSE **TRE-FOEL** HOME OF THE BARE HILL **MOEL DINMAEL** BARE HILL OF THE CHIEF'S FORT **TY-AR-Y-GRAIG** HOUSE ON THE ROCK **TRE-GWYNT** WINDY HOMESTEAD **TY FAENOR** STONE HOUSE OF THE CHIEFTAN **LLUESTCERRIG** HILL FARM OF THE STONES **MOCHDRE** HOMESTEAD OF THE PIGS **PANTYNEUADD** HOLLOW OF THE HALL **LLUESTDDUALLT** CABIN OF THE BLACK SLOPE **GWAUM TRE BEDDAU** MOOR OF THE HOME OF GRAVES **TRE'R-DDÔL** HOMESTEAD OF THE MEADOW **PEN LLUESTY CARN** HEAD OF THE CABIN OF THE CAIRN **TREGRUGYN** HOMESTEAD OF THE SMALL CAIRN **TREHELIG-GRO** WILLOW HOME OF PEBBLES **FACH-WEN** FAIR NOOK **DISGWYLFA** A WATCHING PLACE **TREBERFYDD** HOMESTEAD IN THE MIDDLE-LAND **FELINDRE** HOME OF THE VILLEINS **TY-BRITH** MOTTLED HOUSE **TY-CRWYN** HOUSE OF SKINS **LLAWR BETWS** BEAD-HOUSE ON LOW GROUND **LLUEST DÔL GWIAIL** CABIN OF THE MEADOW OF CANES **TRE-HAIDD** HOMESTEAD OF BARLEY **TAIRDERWEN** THREE HOUSES OF THE OAK **TY DANYDDERWEN** HOUSE UNDER THE OAK TREE **TREDERWEN FEIBION** HOME OF THE OAK OF THE SONS **TRE-WERN** HOMESTEAD OF MARSH ALDERS **TYN-Y-TWLL** COTTAGE OF THE HOLE **TREFNANNAU** HOMESTEAD OF THE STREAMS **TYLWCH** HOUSE OF MUD, HOME NEAR THE POOL **GOETRE-FAWR** HOME IN THE BIG WOOD **TYN-Y-BYRWYDD** COTTAGE OF THE SHORT WOOD **PENTRE-HWNT** YONDER VILLAGE **TREALAW** HOME OF SONG **PENTRE'R-BEIRDD** VILLAGE OF THE POETS **DISERTH** WILDERNESS RETREAT **EISTEDDFA** RESTING PLACE **TO BACH** LITTLE ROOF **TY-POETH** WARM HOUSE **DIHEWYD** PLEASANT PLACE **TALWEN** FAIR END

Cartref Caret

Helveti(c)a

ET IN ARCADIA TIBICINE EST

THE TREES ARE ALL IN ORDER

DORIC

IONIC

CORINTHIAN

Et in Arcadia Tibicine Est

I've always worked with words. After lengthy spells pressing them into the service of others' interests, I returned them to serving my own creative practice, but had concerns my instinctive passion for language-referent art and visual literature would likely leave me outside any group that might share my interest and encourage my endeavour.

I first met Steven J Fowler in 2017, when he brought Writers' Centre Kingston into its surrounding community, and I was expanding my engagement with the broader creative population. Our collaboration at The Museum of Futures I'd helped establish as a safe, stimulating local space for creative energy and ideas to thrive seems a prescient prefiguring of my participation in PoPoGrou. Four busily productive years partnering Writers' Centre at the Museum and across the capital expanded my community and the permissions I knew I never really needed to be as productive as I'd always hoped and offered access to the support and resources I needed to explore sharing the work I make more widely.

When by necessity we all went online, I found myself far from alone but in the even broader safe embrace of a generous, inclusive, unconventional and celebratory community of remarkable creative and productive folk, whose progressive goodwilled practise has since been profoundly contributing to my creative evolution. PoPoGrou. It's been a joyful privilege to find such a rare depth of friendship and fellowship across this rich and supportive ecosystem of practitioners – engaged and inquisitive folk bearing witness to each other's immersion in what Steven's captured as 'language art where the miracle of language itself can be turned away from expediency […] which does not necessarily aim to be informative or communicative […] a burst of the miraculous'.

I wouldn't be the productive poet I am now, living the vivid life I lead, without these beautiful beings and the PoPoGrou story in my life.

PoPoGrou is a story about my peeroes.

CAMERON
WADE

Cameron Wade is a London-based writer and poet. His work currently explores textual, visual, collaborative and prose poetry, as well as science fiction and flash fiction. In his spare time, he is an amateur astronomer and history buff. The National Gallery has commissioned his work and, in 2023, his debut chapbook *I Smell Metal* was published by Sampson Low.

```
I  T  '  S  T  H  E  S  I  Z  E  A  N
D  S  H  A  P  E  A  N  D  M  A  S  S
O  F  D  I  S  A  P  P  O  I  N  T  M
E  N  T  F  O  L  D  E  D  B  E  T  W
E  E  N  T  H  E  T  W  I  S  T  S  O
F  A  P  A  G  E  F  R  O  M  T  H  E
R  E  D  R  A  F  T  O  F  D  I  V  O
R  C  E  P  R  O  C  E  E  D  I  N  G
S  S  L  I  P  P  E  D  S  N  U  G  G
L  Y  I  N  S  I  D  E  T  H  E  V  A
C  U  O  U  S  E  X  P  A  N  S  E  .
C  U  R  V  E  D  D  E  G  R  E  E  S
O  F  F  R  E  E  D  O  M  C  O  N  F
I  N  E  I  N  T  E  R  A  C  T  I  O
N  S  T  O  I  N  E  R  T  I  A  A  N
D  P  A  U  S  E  T  H  E  A  R  R  O
W  T  O  G  R  E  E  T  T  H  E  R  E
V  E  R  E  N  T  F  I  R  M  A  M  E
N  T  S  C  O  M  M  A  N  D  .  I  T
'  S  A  L  L  F  O  R  W  A  R  D  .
I  T  A  K  E  A  S  T  E  P  D  O  W
N  D  I  A  G  O  N  A  L  L  Y  .
```

Dimensions (3D)

```
         IT'STHESIZEAN
        DISTH'ASPTEHAENSDIMZAESASN
        ODISDHIASPTEHAENODIMKAESMSN
        EONISDHIOSEIDHAEDOBIKETTMSN
        EEGNISDHEASEIBHAEDOBTEXTTMSN
        FEAGDITHHEASPTBHAGHMODEKEETMSN
        RFEAGDIIDHIOSEIBHADHOBTKETDSMSA
        RRGEAGDIIDHIOSEIOBHADHOBTKETDSMSN
        SRRBEEGDIIDHISSEIOBHFADHSDTKETDSMSN
        LSKRFEEGDIIDHIOSEIOBHADHSDTKSTDSSMSN
        CLGKBFEEGDIIDHIOSEIOBHADHSDTKSTDSMSN
        CCDSKGFEEGDIIDHIOSEIOBHADHSDTKSTDSMSN
        OCGLBKGFEEGDIIDHIOSEIOBHADHSDTKSTDSMSN
        IONGBSKGFEEGDIIDHIOSEIOBHADHSDTKSTDSMSN
        NIGHFBDIKGFEEGDIIDHIOSEIOBHADHSDTKSTDSMSN
        DNPGASBBDIKGFEEGDIIDHIOSEIOBHADHSDTKSTDSTSN
        WDWPGASBBDIKGFEEGDIIDHIOSEIOBHADHSDTKSTDSMSN
        VWDNPGASBBDIKGFEEGDIIDHIOSEIOBHADHSDTKSTDSMSN
        NVWDNPGASBBDIKGFEEGDIIDHIOSEIOBHADHSDTKSTDSSN
        'NGWDSPGASBBDIKGFEEGDIIDHIOSEIOBHADHSDTKSTDSMSN
        I'NGTDMBGASBBDIKGFEEGDIIDHIOSEIOBHADHSDTKSTDSMSN
        NIDSGTDMBGASBBDIKGFEEGDIIDHIOSEIOBHADHSDTKSTDSMSN
        NIDTNTDMBGASBBDIKGFEEGDIIDHIOSEIOBHADHSDTKSTDSMSN
        NIDTNTDMBGASBBDIKGFEEGDIIDHIOSEIOBHADHSDTKSTDSMSN
        NIDTNTKNDBGASBBDIKGFEEGDIIDHIOSEIOBHADHSDTKSTDSMSN
        NIDTNITKNDBGASBBDIKGFEEGDIIDHIOSEIOBHADHSDTKSTDSMSN
        NIDTNTKNDBGASBBDIKGFEEGDIIDHIOSEIOBHADHSDTKSTDSMS
        NIDTNTKNDBGASBBDIKGFEEGDIIDHIOSEIOBHADHSDTKSTOWM
        NIDTNTKNDBGASBBDIKGFEEGDIIDHIOSEIOBHADHSDTKSTOW
        NIDTNTKNDBGASBBDIKGFEEGDIIDHIOSEIOBHADHSXTHGEO
        NIDTNTKNDBGASBBDIKGFEEGDIIDHIOSEIOBHADHETTUHOE
        NIDTNTKNDBGASBBDIKGFEEGDIIDHIOSEIKNBBEGNUGO
        NIDTNTKNDBGASBBDIKGFEEGDIIDHIOSEIBEECAGG
        NIDTNTKNDBGASBBDIKGFEEGDIIDHIRHESBEYGAG
        NIDWNTKNDBGASBBDIKGFEEGDIIDHBERRBENGES.A
        NIDWNTKNDBGASBBDIKGFEEGDIIRARBENGES.
        NIDNTNTNDBGASBBDIKGFEEGEIRRKODNGFS
        NIDWTTKNDBGASBBDIKGFEEICBHDGARRRESTMOF
        NIDWTTDMBGASBBDIKGFEEIXBESAERRREDNO
        NIDWTTKNDBGASBBDIKGFEEOKNDKESAERRREON
        NIDWTNTKNDBGASBBDIKGFEEDYIDHWDERRREO
        NIDWTTKNSSGGONKNAEDEDYIDWGAEKTEE
        NIDWTKAERGDONKSMRBEENKDMODWMTE
        NIDWSTAGGCDONKMTRBEENKDRODW.T
        NIDTSAAKGEDANSOTREEPKDRODW.
        NIDTIAAKGEOANSATLELPYD.O W
             NDIAGONALLY.
```

Dimensions (4D)

The Hours (bottled)

Washed up on
a paved shore that
sticks against a thieving tide, where
loathsome to wander passers-by slide
with the urgency of chalk,
the blind eye of geology. Cracked,
abandoned and green
in daylight I wonder,
        what are you blown from?
        What did you contain?

MARTIN
WAKEFIELD

Martin Wakefield is a poet from London. His most recent book, a collection of visual poetry called *Propositions. Autobiography.*, was published by Moormaid Press in November 2023. Previous books include *Zugunruhe* (2019), *Jungle Gym* (2021) and *Poems You Can't Colour In* (2023) from Hesterglock Press, *Emptpy Poems* from Sampson Low (2022), and *Handsfree*, a collaboration with Bob Modem (Paul Hawkins), from Steel Incisors (2023). His work has been published in *3:AM Magazine*, *Osmosis Press*, *Poem Atlas* and *Idler Magazine* amongst others, and anthologised by Trickhouse Press, KU Press, Steel Incisors, Penteract Press and Hesterglock Press.

Déjà vécu

oi! the present form
constitutes a prompt
to set you in flow
the editor and
author reserve all
rights for illinformed
potential misuse
the chosen pieces

which are presented
have so developed

an environment which creates the most excellent
conditions for real substantial and intellectual
activity an individual stance towards quantity
will also shape the interactional quality
of each piece and the rain the rain will fall come what may
rupturing gutters buttering pavements straking glass
polishing the withdrawn surface of all things solid
Xenodice covers his ears Pasiphaë smiles while
alexithymic Sid climbs onto his sodden cot
and miniates the silvered world (upon the earth of
all flesh the dust mired the ooze will scab the earth orange
the red earth the substance will be forever destroyed)

Jhonny
canoes
to the
end of
the pier

Pasiphaë holds two phials up to the fading light (under the pretext of
sending gifts to children the prisoners put their sperm into empty pen tubes
and hide them inside chocolate bars) (a narrative text which garners power to
itself by manipulating the reader into thinking that narration
prevails over diegesis prevails over mimesis on the road to
the unspoken we trigger the limits of societal norms as a site

of performance or spectropoetics so that these handpainted birds circling
overhead represent the kaleidoscopic self which strives to unravel
the layers of metamorphosis from human to divine liberation)

steel plus zinc thus galvanised steel plus oxygen thus zinc oxide plus
hydrogen thus zinc hydroxide plus carbon dioxide and thus zinc
carbonate in his hut on his cot Sid is oblivious to the
deafening roar from the stadium sound swelled into a description
defying triumphal ritualistic chant with arms raised Charlie George
races across the pitch hair streaming as he hears his admiring fans
greet yet another fantastic goal like happy inmates suddenly

ghosts

Déjà rêvé

he took his toco well I must say Nanc but is it he has a lurking walk
and as he walks constantly looks over his shoulder first on one side and
    then on the other is it his eyes
are sunk in his head so much deeper than any other man's is it his face is
    dark like his
hair and eyes and although he can't be more than one or two and twenty
    withered and haggard is
it his lips are often discoloured and disfigured with the marks of teeth is it
    he has fits
desperate and degrading and sometimes even bites his hands and covers
    them with wounds is it
the pages of his philosophy books are stained with dried blood is it he says
    fuck the second
law of thermodynamics they show penis gourds the teds from the Tyne
    and so our convictions

dissipate upon the waters dark and rude so how much longer would we
    idly rest and stay
contemplating the endlessly shifting deserts between dry memory and
    atrophied place

this phial
(there were two
now there's one
what do you
mean there's no
con to ret)
contains the
sanctified
spunk of my
beloved
bull you'll use
it to birth

that pair of
cursed Cretan
boppers Jim

and Martin
(there'll be no

stopping them
hopping no)
Daedalus
(the old fraud)
told me X
will leave you
Sid will die
you'll need hope
(there is none)

up in the
attic the
buckets plink
confusion
we need to
get out of
here Xeno

dark matter

Die Überlebenden

and there was
always a
thing and then
a space then
another
thing and this could be a body a

book a cup
a dagger

this appeal is clear the reader of poems is youthful language this appeal
is clear the reader of poems falling on deaf ears and yet independent
of all doctrine this appeal is clear the transforming action of poetic
imagination all the disciplined schools of thought at the level of the
poetic image the duality of subject and object is ever
iridescent and shimmering unceasingly active in the reader of
poems countless experiments profited by the transforming action of
poetic imagination and to measure the total product of that
consciousness poetic images are content in their immobility
it seems they have no consequences as is too the case with the transforming
action of poetic imagination understandable by all this
in virtue of embodying the transsubjectivity of the image

for example the word Löwe (lion) occurs once
only in the German language is identical
throughout its innumerable utterances by
all given persons whereas the assertion of a
geometrical object is never thematic

we are like poetic lines
being woven into prose
Jhonny says Xenodice
a combination of text
and image that leaves the
doors open for opinion
imagination and thought
and explores the intimate
endogenous ambience

living wakefully in the world we are constantly aware of eus wrotid whether
    we pay
attention or are not conscious of it the borizon of
our lie as a horizon of things (real objects etc and so on and so forth) and so
    Jhonny commences countdown
(the old impossible machine) and as he and Xeno leave for Europe after the
    rain P
squats and gives him nascency and there are angels with fireworks for wings
    who stamp their feet and shriek
six six for my sorrow seven seven for no tomorrow eight I forget what eight
    was for
but nine nine for the lost gods and ten ten for everything everything
    everything

(let's skip darling Sid
it was only an
'opeless fancy it
passed like an April
day but a look an'
a word an' the dreams
they stirred you 'ave stole
my hear' righ' away)

1   isolation means being visited by one's own ghosts.

1.1   you are not yourself when you are alone.

2   to achieve selfhood you must appear.

2.1   and do.

2.1.1   and doing entails relationship.

2.1.1.1 and relationship entails open collaboration and sometimes open disagreement.

3   this is how we come to be ourselves in the Popogrou family.

LORI
WIKE

Lori Wike is a musician and writer based in Salt Lake City, Utah. Her work has been published in *Reflections*, *The Book of Penteract*, and *Seen as Read*, and her first full-length puzzle poetry book *Jump Search* was published by Penteract Press in 2023. Her writings can also be found in the journals *Word Ways*, *Anamorphoseis*, *InVisibleCulture*, *aswirl*, and *The Journal of Wordplay*. She is principal bassoon of the Utah Symphony and teaches at the University of Utah and Westminster University.

X: @lori_wike

On the Psychology of Roller Coasters
(Palindrome-Calligramme)

Deep-spun upset, a torpor dips. Agile vertebra, oscillate manipulative lap bar. Glee, ride pools, track carts looped, I reel! Grab pale vital up in a metallic soar! Bet revel I gasp, I drop! Rotate, spun-up speed!

One Line Haiku

ID LEERED, THERE ALCHEMISTS SWEPT

The one-line haiku consists of a single line of black and red text. It could be considered as a kind of minimalist puzzle haiku or perhaps just an economical use of letters: this particular haiku uses only 28 letters.

The single line above contains seven syllables and is the middle line of the haiku. The text in red consists of insider words within the longer line and is the first five-syllable line of the haiku. The leftover letters in black contain the third line of the haiku and also consist of five syllables.

The one-line haiku above would thus be read as:

IDLE RED MIST WEPT
ID LEERED, THERE ALCHEMISTS SWEPT
ETHEREAL CHESS

ERODE
RENAMED
REMEMBER
OWNSTORE
CHA A A
CONFUSED
ANTARES
STADT

Remember confused remnants, embossed.

From FRAGMENTS OF A CHEQUERED PAST

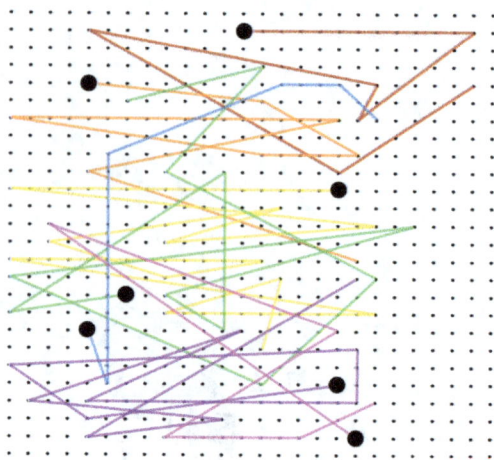

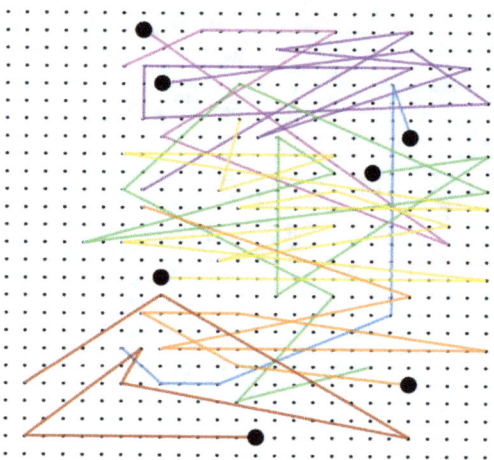

Two titles from ARIADNE

An asemic-cryptographic set of puzzle dominoes

136

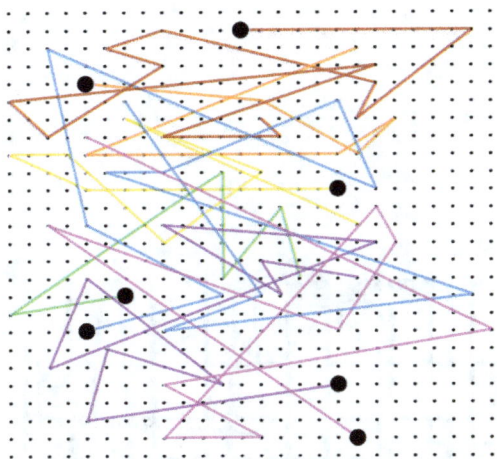

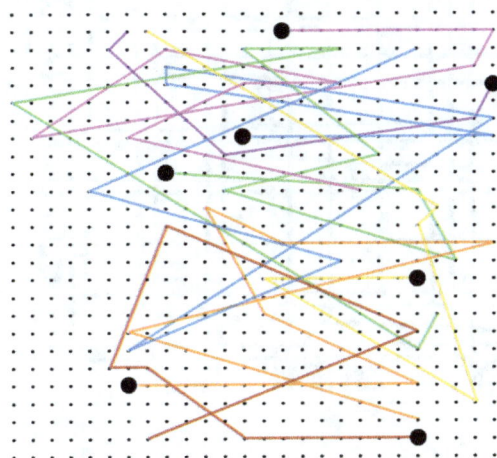

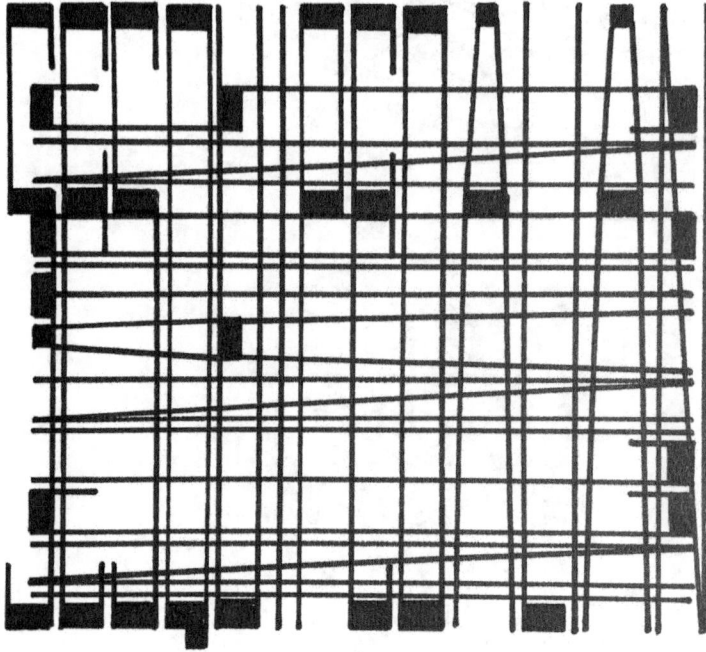

Sesquipedalian Inclinations

HTSKKTT

Hamlet Soliloquy Quartet of Unvoiced Consonants
in Simple Canon
(Each new unvoice begins at the asterisk)

T T T T K ST *

WH T T S F

S T S F T

T T K ST S T

P T T S P

S P T S

H T K TH T SH KS

T F SH T T K S SH

T T SH T T S P

T S P P CH S T

F T S P TH WH T K

WH SH F F S T K

ST S P SP KT

T KS K T S F

F WH WH PS SK T

P S P K T

P S

S S F S SP

T P SH T T T KS

WH H H S F T H K T S K

TH K WH F

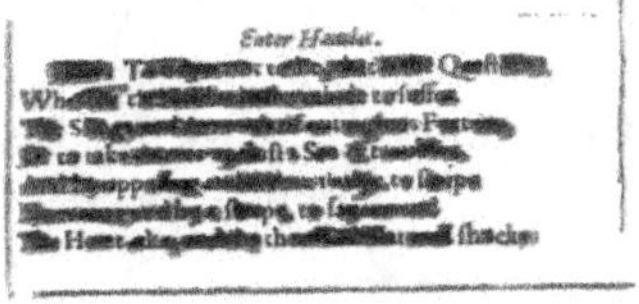

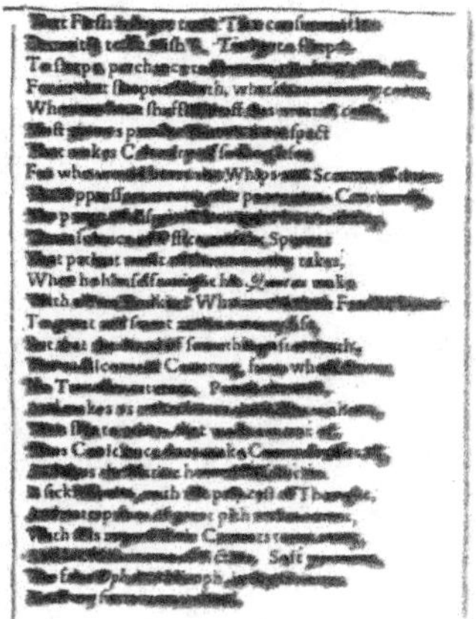

T T S T F

T T S TH FT TH

SK K T F WH

T T P

KS S H

F T T T

S K SH S K K S

S T H SH

S K TH P K ST TH T

T P T P CH T

TH S K TS T

KSH S FT

F F F

S

HTSKKTT from Hamlet Soliloquy Quartet
a sound poetry suite of 3 pieces

Vital Statistics

Identity: Pink Floyd, flamingo escapee

Genus: Phoenicopterus roseus

Origins: Tracy Aviary, Liberty Park, Salt Lake City, UT

Hatching: A non-traditional rose tincture without a designated heraldic pattern

Year Escaped: 1976

Reason for Escape: Aviary procedural failure in wing-clipping

Wintering Grounds: Shores of the Great Salt Lake

Summering Grounds: Kingston upon Thames

Habitat Companions: Gulls; waterfowl; brine shrimp. In the early 2000s, a group calling themselves Friends of Floyd petitioned the governor of Utah to bring 25 flamingos to Great Salt Lake to join Floyd. Ten life-sized flamingo replicas were planted along the shoreline to garner public support, but the plan was nixed by the Utah Division of Wildlife Resources. Finally, in the early 2020s, a Fowler-led campaign successfully established the rogue flamingo collective known as Popogrou. This collectivity-without-captivity imposed no geographical or procedural limitations beyond the labyrinths created by the flamingos themselves.

Designated Collective Noun: While a flock of flamingos was traditionally referred to as a flamboyance, in honor of Fowler's remarkable measures and the resulting flock's flights and feats of fancy, the preferred term is now a Popogrou.

PoPoGrou

ACKNOWLEDGEMENTS

As there is currently no prescribed way of rendering the collective's name in text – it has, equally acceptably, appeared as Popogrou, popogrou and PoPoGrou, amongst others – it is to what the introduction refers to as the 'grand set of poets who loosely collect under eight letters' that we offer our considerable heartfelt thanks here:

Lisa Blackwell, Bob Brightt, Susie Campbell, Patrick Cosgrove, Laura Davis, Steven J Fowler, Beverly Frydman, Lucy Furlong, Sylee Gore, Carolyn Hashimoto, Ailsa Holland, Vicki Kaye, Mark Rutter, Jules Sprake, Stephen Sunderland, Simon Tyrrell, Cameron Wade, Martin Wakefield and Lori Wike.

This collection of beautifully brilliant work would not have been possible without the friendship and fellowship of the remarkable people it celebrates, and their enabling and generous support for the editor during its evolution.

We would also like to acknowledge Chris Kerr's long-term contribution to the collective's endeavours, if not, sadly, the pages here – his absence is a result of circumstance not inclination, and his presence in our midst here is sorely missed.

Popogrou would neither be, nor have become anything, without Steven J Fowler. Thank you for all things, dear friend.

You would not have this in your hands without the patient commitment of Emma Tait and the team of Kingston University students pursuing their masters in publishing to bring the anthology alive. Thank you, Alana Applewhaite, Kara Daniel, Emma Fisher and Julieta Pereyra, for working so tirelessly with us to produce something of which we can all be proud.

ABOUT KU PRESS

Kingston University Press has been publishing high-quality commercial and academic titles for over ten years. Our list has always reflected the diverse nature of the student and academic bodies at the university in ways that are designed to impact on debate, to hear new voices, to generate mutual understanding and to complement the values to which the university is committed.

Increasingly the books we publish are produced by students on the Kingston School of Art MA courses, often working with partner organisations to bring projects to life. While keeping true to our original mission, and maintaining our wide-ranging backlist titles, our most recent publishing focuses on bringing to the fore voices that reflect and appeal to our community at the university as well as the wider reading community of readers and writers in the UK and beyond.

@KU_press

This book was edited, designed, typeset and produced by students on the Kingston School of Art MA courses at Kingston University, London.

To find out more about our hands-on, professionally focused and flexible MA and BA programmes please visit:

www.kingston.ac.uk

www.kingstonpublishing.wordpress.com

@kingstonjourno

www.ingramcontent.com/pod-product-compliance
Lightning Source LLC
LaVergne TN
LVHW022341080426
835508LV00012BA/1295